HY

GASTRIC BAND

Stop Food Addiction and Eat Healthy with Rapid Weight Loss Hypnosis. Self Esteem, Confidence, Meditation, Deep Sleep, Past Life Regression, and Positive Affirmations for Women

YOUNAN CAMPBELL

TABLE OF CONTENTS

Introduction

The gastric band (also called a lap band) has become an increasingly popular treatment for people who want to lose weight over the course of the last decade. A band is wrapped around the stomach and inflated to reduce the stomach capacity greatly. It means that the patient consumes less food, resulting in fast and permanent weight loss.

Yet gastric band surgery is not risk-free. There is always an inherent risk of something going wrong with any procedure, but there are also some problems that the lap band can cause in particular. It involves a ribbon (which may lead to too much or not enough stomach capability), acid reflux, nausea, vomiting, diarrhea, regurgitation, blockages as well as other problems. There are definitely hidden dangers, although the results are certainly impressive. But wouldn't it be awesome if the performance of the gastric band could be repeated without risks?

Okay, there's actually away. Hypnotherapists recently succeeded tremendously in replicating the lap band solely with hypnotic suggestions. No scalpels, anesthetics, or wounds - just pure mind control. Because of its safe and effective existence, gastric belt hypnotherapy has become the newest weight-loss craze. A simple search of Google shows hundreds of happy patients who benefit from hypnotherapy of the gastric band and lose much of their excess weight. How does it work, however?

To order to understand how gastric band hypnotherapy functions, we first need to consider hypnosis and the effect on the mind. The most logical hypothesis is that, though human knowledge of the mind is far from total, the mind contains two main components-the conscious and the subconscious. You will be better familiar with the concept of the conscious mind, as this is the basis of your daily thinking pattern. Each time you think "I'm thirsty, I should go have a drink" or something similar that works in your conscious mind. The unconscious mind is, in a sense, much darker and stronger. This regulates all these instinctive behaviors and reactions, your habits, your impulses, and your phobia you do not even know about. The subconscious mind is working on hypnosis. Hypnosis prevails and prepares the subconscious to accept suggestions.

Since we understand how hypnosis works, how gastric band hypnotherapy works is a little easier. A hypnotherapist takes his client to a hypnotic state and then speaks about them as if it actually happens via the gastric band technique. There is no real pain or painful occurrence, but fantasy and reality are difficult to distinguish from the subconscious mind. That's why sometimes really strong dreams seem too real.

Once the subconscious mind thinks the body is fitted with a gastric band, it is as if you really have one. It ensures that you will feel better, eat more, and eat smaller foods. It obviously leads to a very significant loss of weight.

In addition to being better than surgery, gastric band hypnotherapy is also much more cost-effective-ten times lower than surgery. There are also audio services that are provided by professional hypnotherapists that are exactly the same on CD or MP3, which are still less expensive as the hypnotherapist only has to record the session once for certain clients. It could cost less than $100.

Therefore, if you think of a gastric band procedure, the natural hypnotherapy approach might well be worth considering.

Gastric band hypnosis is a process that makes very creative use of the imagination of an individual. This is an innovative form in hypnotherapy that has attracted much media attention and very positive ads in the European and English papers. And this is part of this procedure's elegance. It catches the imagination of all. And that is what hypnotherapy and hypnotherapy or hypnotics are all about at its heart. Capture your vision.

Do all hypnotists and hypnotherapists perform this kind of hypnotic weight loss? No. No. This is a new process which started as a concept to help a customer regain control of their appetite. They wanted a reason to stop eating. So they wanted a more concrete reason than the long-term benefit that they could lose weight by following a healthier diet. What more should you than a really negative physical reaction to eating too much? And that's what happens when you hypnotically mount the gastric band. The clients should feel physically full and stop eating quickly.

Any hypnotic or hypnotherapist who works will learn the techniques to help their patients lose weight. The creators of this idea experimented with various methods and found what produced the best results. And when you know which way to help weight loss clients achieve their target, you will have an effective referral-based hypnotherapy practice.

The interested hypnotherapist has several training options. Some of them are distance learning, where you can get written instructions about what to say and when to say. Some are just a one-session recording. And then there are the few in a classroom setting. The final option provides you with an ability to ask questions and an insight into how this process will work for you and your customers.

When you are trained in gastric hypnosis, you can learn how to use the imagination of your client to get control of their diet and activities. You will even teach your customers how to handle the feelings behind their weight problems. An innovative training program for hypnotists and hypnotherapists will provide you with the exact scripts to help your clients to overcome their weight problems and to give them a powerful resource that will automatically improve their responses to the amount of food they eat.

And as most effective training sessions teach you how to deal with emotional reasons your customers eat too much, your customers create new rules to improve your wellbeing.

There has been a lot of news coverage of the virtual hypnotic gastric band recently, but does this work? The vast number of websites out there will make you believe it works and is reliable.

Sure there were reports in the newspapers, but are these not press releases sent to such outlets to make this practice more credible?

There won't be a newspaper writing an article stating that the hypnotic gastric band doesn't work because who would read it? It would be like publishing an article that states that children don't like to eat vegetables. However, if you published an article which states that a new technique was invented to make children love vegetables, it would be a different story.

Nevertheless, the only outlets that can talk with certainty about whether a technique works or not are scientific journals reviewed by peers. Since this technique was on the market, there were no scientific papers proving the effectiveness of the virtual hypnotic gastric band.

This method of weight loss does not vary from weight-loss operations that you assume to have the solution to your weight problem. We want you to believe that their treatment can instantly remove the mental and physiological factors that produce your weight problem today. For a fact, no treatment can do this if it doesn't address the real reasons why you have a weight problem.

Another such operation is much like cutting off the head of a plant. At first, you think it's gone, and you're making progress, but those roots under the ground continue to

13

pine for the sun. Then slowly, they start to break the surface of the soil and start to take over again your old behavior patterns. Maybe then you say to yourself that because you were so good, you deserve this chocolate bar. At the end of the day, the weeds continue to bloom and take over more of your lawn, and you stop trying to lose weight.

The hypnotic band may help some people temporarily lose weight, but people start extending the limits of this procedure over time, some of which are related to the actual operating version. The only thing about the emotional and physiological aspects of over-alimentation is that they will come back again if they are not treated. This may be at one time when a person is under emotional stress. The person can then use food as a comfort consciously or unconsciously.

The person returns then to the belief that they have a gastric band installed after this incident, but that a small slip has undermined this belief. The next time the person undergoes some emotional stress, then it is easier for them to use food for warmth, as they did it in the past.

Then the individual doesn't believe in a gastric band and resorts to the emotional and physiological aspects of overfeeding, which have never really been dealt within the first place. The person can choose to buckle another £1,200 for some places to do it again.

The mental and physiological factors that lead to overweight need to be overcome to be truly successful not only in the short-term but also in the long term. Then, by solving these things, no real or imagined procedure is required because the roots of the problem are no longer present.

Diet means not eating anything today. This is different from what it used to say. It was what you used to eat. But it's changed so that you're limited, restricted, and stopped what you want.

To successfully diet, you have to do one thing. Concentrate on what you want and what's good for your body. You should read all the articles where one paper says that chocolate is good for you, and another paper says it is good for you. It happens again because we are actually. Some people can have chocolate, and it doesn't have any effect. Some just seem to want it, and their body doesn't help at all.

The best way to eat is for the body to feed. One way to do this is by muscle monitoring or kinesiology. This approach checks your muscles to decide whether something influences the energy field of your body. If it hurts, don't have it. If it doesn't interfere, you can get it. You just check what you're intolerant of.

When you know what you can eat, you eat it and avoid it when you're thirsty. You will raise your weight whether you eat maximum or not hungry. Therefore, concentrate on regulating your eating behavior and consuming what you think is good for your body, and it will be your effective diet.

So, identify the pattern of your eating. What does your body tell you to do and not to do? First, build the eating behavior you like. Identify if you can't have anything. If you have one, you have a preference as to whether or not you have one. Otherwise, as long as it fits your body, you can have food. So, forget all those other diets out and create your own.

If you would like to lose some weight without using surgery, then the hypnotic gastric band is the best tool for you. The hypnotic gastric band is the natural healthy eating tool that will help to control your appetite and your portion sizes. In this sense, hypnosis plays a significant role in helping you to lose weight without having to go through the risk that comes with surgery.

It is a subconscious suggestion that you already have, a gastric band comes intending to influence the body to respond by creating a feeling of satiety. It is now available in a public domain that dieting does not help to solve lifestyle challenges that are needed for weight loss and management.

Temporary diet plans are not effective while maintaining continuous plans are difficult. Notably, these plans are going to deprive you of your favorite foods, since they're too restrictive. Deep down within you, you might have a problem with your body's weight since diets have not worked for you in the past.

If you want to try something that will be able to provide a positive edge for you, then you should be able to control your cravings around food hypnotically. By reaching this point, you must try hypnosis, which has proven some results in aiding weight loss.

Benefits of hypnosis vs. surgery

If you would like to lose weight without starvation or yo-yo dieting, then the hypnotic gastric band is the ultimate resort for you. This gastric band does not require surgery but only meditation and hypnosis. Therefore, it offers numerous benefits that make it the solution to rapid weight loss and craving healthy food.

It is pain-free: As opposed to the physical gastric band, the hypnotic gastric band does not require surgery, which is associated with pain and routine follow-ups. Therefore, you do not need to worry about the risks you need to take, as no physical operation will be done on your body. You only need to hypnotize and utilize the hypnosis to work on your body weight.

100% safe: As hypnosis is a non-invasive, non-surgical, and safe technique, so is the hypnotic gastric band whose mechanism is initiated in your subconscious mind. Through the practice, there are no expected dangers, and you learn about self-awareness and the course of your life.

Time-efficient: You do not need to wait for your vacation to acquire a hypnotic gastric band. The tool does not affect your schedule as hypnosis can be combined with most of your day to day activities. You do not need time off to adjust the band or report complications

No meal replacement or dieting: With the hypnotic gastric band, you do not need to stop eating your most enjoyable food. Instead, you develop a principle that makes you feel in control and enable you to lose weight consistently and naturally without dieting. You just exercise and unlock the power in you to make positive changes in life.

No complications: The fact that no surgery is performed in hypnotic gastric surgery puts away the worry about future complications. The ease in your mind plays a significant role in focusing your mind on the things that matter, such as visualization and meditation. This way, you can put off negative thinking and live your life fearlessly and positively.

Helps discover your hidden potential: The use of hypnosis and meditation makes you learn about how to utilize the power of your mind in changing your perception and erasing negative thoughts. Similarly, you become capable of helping not only with weight loss but also with other psychological and social aspects such as confidence. In this case, hypnosis helps plant a subconscious suggestion in your mind making it stick and become a strong idea.

Cost-Effective: Hypnotic gastric band does not snatch away your working time, making you fully productive at your workplace with no deductions. In the same way, there are no costs in hypnosis and meditation as opposed to the physical gastric band. Positively living your life substantially adds to your savings.

Weight loss through hypnosis

Now, as I am walking down the beach, I will come to an area with unpleasant bells written by me in the sand. Those labels have been given to me in the past. Those labels are the labels that have held me back in the past from reaching my true capacity and from reaching my true power. I see those labels in the sand, and I begin to use my leg to clean them and use my legs to wash it off and clean the area with sweeping. With my feet, I erase the words away with every stroke of my feet, and I watch as the water comes to the shore to clear them away and clear all this around me.

Those words mean nothing to me; they do not exist again because I was the only one that saw them. I turn them around, and I work a little way down the beach. I feel more confident and taller. I come to the middle of a large rock sitting in the middle of the sand, and on this rock, there is a little pick. I pick it up, and I begin to write all the things that I want about my life. I begin to write all the things that I want about my weight. I am writing all the things that describe me. I am writing that I am confident, I am talented, and I am accomplished. And that I am a good person. I write as many words as possible that describe me.

I write things like positive, attractive, and capable I look at all the words that I have written on this rock and I know that I am a great person. I begin to recall all the moments whereby I felt confident. I think of the time that I felt confident, and I recall those feelings again. I visualize those convenient moments in my life, and what it felt like, what it sounded like, and I then realize what it smells like. I believe this positive moment in my life. I think of the times where I felt confident in my life.

I feel those feelings. I picture those moments again, and I make the colors brighter and more vivid. I feel those feelings of confidence and pride, and I turn off the sounds and the smells. I get back into those moments where I was feeling so confident and powerful that I was feeling so confident in myself and all the things that I was doing. I am confident in the way I look. I am confident in the way I dress, and I'm confident in the way I act. I am confident in my relationship. I am confident in the relationship that I have with the members of the opposite sex. I am confident in the relationship that I have with my family with my friends and my coworkers.

Things come to me easily, with the way I talk to people. Conversations come out fluently from my mouth, and people respect what I have to say. I am strong and respected, and everyone around me sees me as confident and capable I take a look at myself, and I see that I am full of positive energy. I am the one that is radiating how everyone sees me. Everyone around me sees the positive energy in me, not only the people around me, but I also respect myself. I stand tall and strong. I stand proud of myself. I know that I can accomplish whatever I put my mind to accomplish. All I am seeing are positive things in my life.

I have practical and creative ideas, and I fill my mind with positive energy. I drop the future and go forward with confidence. I imagine myself one year from now, and I imagine the person that I will grow up to be. When I imagine this image, I will not be able to recognize the person that I once was. I have accomplished great things in the past year, great things that will help me to reach my capabilities.

My confidence has enabled others to look at me with great confidence and respect. I enjoy talking with people, and they're interested in what I have to say. My career is going great, and I can voice my ideas and opinions to other people because they value them. The relationship with my friends and families are great. Most of my friends and families come to seek advice from me because they hold me in high esteem. I look at myself, and I see how positive I am. I can point others in the right direction that they should go. I have faith in myself. I have great ideas, and I know that my family and friends respect my ideas, and they know my values too. I hold my head high, and I know that nothing can bring me down. I stand tall and strong because I know that I am an accomplished, beautiful, capable, and confident person.

Why it works

Normally, the conscious mind is receptive to suggestions, because it normally analyzes it.

With hypnosis, you will be able to reach your desired weight, become healthier, and stay in shape for life with the right mindset. You will be able to empower your mind to accept suggestions in a deep and relaxed state. This way, you will be able to reframe your thinking patterns because of all the principles of suggestion and disassociation. With the hypnotic gastric band, you will be able to use suggestions to influence a different response from your body triggered by sensory data to be able to create a new reality. The suggestions will be to provide a guideline for you to follow without questioning or critiquing.

Ultimately, this power will be able to allow you to reframe and reshape your perception regarding a specific behavior. The complex network in your brain has many different interpretations of the world around you, and the most unhelpful and negative thoughts have worked their way into that network.

Thus, you become susceptible to uncontrolled unconscious urges, like overeating and ignoring bodyweight concerns. Hypnotic gastric band will help you to be able to dampen and overcome all those uncontrolled thoughts, believes, and suggestions that are helping you alter your behavior.

Chapter 2: Conditioning Your Body for Hypnotic Gastric Band

The physical gastric band requires a surgical procedure that involves reducing the size of your stomach pocket to accommodate less volume of food and as a result of the stretching of the walls of the stomach, send signals to the brain that you are filled and therefore need to stop eating any further.

The hypnotic gastric band also works in the same manner, although in this case, the only surgical tools you will be needing are your mind and your body, and the great part is, you can conduct the procedure yourself. The hypnotic gastric band also conditions your mind and body to restrict excess consumption of food after very modest meals. There are three specific differences between the surgical (physical), and hypnotic gastric bands:

In using the hypnotic band, all necessary adjustments are done by continued use of trance.

There is the absence of physical surgery, and therefore you are exposed to no risks at all.

When compared with the surgical gastric band, the hypnotic gastric band is a lot cheaper and easier to do.

The Power of the Gastric Band

A renowned and dramatic case of the power of hypnotic to influence our bodies directly is in the emergency treatment of burns. A few doctors have used hypnotic on many occasions to accelerate and improve the recuperating of extreme injuries and to help reduce the excruciating pains for his patients. If somebody is seriously burnt, there will be damage to the tissue, and the body reacts with inflammation. The patients are hypnotized to forestall the soreness. His patients heal quite rapidly and with less scarring.

There are a lot more instances of how the mind can directly and physically influence the body. We realize that chronic stress can cause stomach ulcers, and a psychological shock can turn somebody's hair to grey color overnight. In any case, what I especially like about this aspect of hypnotism is that it is an archived case of how the mind influences the body positively and medically. It will be somewhat of a miraculous event if the body can get into a hypnotic state that can cause significant physical changes in your body. Hypnotic trance without anyone else has a profound physiological effect. The most immediate effect is that subjects discover it deeply relaxing. Interestingly, the most widely recognized perception that my customers report after I have seen them—regardless of what we have been dealing with—is that their loved ones tell them they look more youthful.

Cybernetic Loop

Your brain and body are in constant correspondence in a cybernetic loop: they continually influence one another. As the mind unwinds in a trance, so too does the body. When the body unwinds, it feels good, and it sends that message to the brain, which thus feels healthier and unwinds much more. This procedure decreases stress and makes more energy accessible to the immune system of the body. It is essential to take note that the remedial effects of hypnotic don't require tricks or amnesia. For example, burns patients realize they have been burnt, so they don't need to deny the glaring evidence of how burnt parts of their bodies are. He essentially hypnotizes them and requests that they envision cool, comfortable sensations over the burnt area. That imaginative activity changes their body's response to the burns.

The enzymes that cause inflammation are not released, and accordingly, the burn doesn't advance to a more elevated level of damage, and there is reduced pain during the healing process.

By using hypnotic and imagery, a doctor can get his patients' bodies to do things that are totally outside their conscious control. Willpower won't make these sorts of changes, but the creative mind is more grounded than the will. By using hypnotic and imagery to talk to the conscious mind, we can have a physiological effect in as little as 20 minutes.

With hypnotic, we can enormously enhance the effect of the mind. When we fit your hypnotic gastric band, it is a way of using the very same strategy of hypnotic correspondence to the conscious mind. We communicate to the brain with distinctive imagery, and the brain alters your body's responses, changing your physical response to food so your stomach is constricted, and you feel truly full after only a few.

A few people think that it's difficult to accept that trance and imagery can have such an extreme and ground-breaking effect. Some doctors were at first distrustful and accepted that his patients more likely than not had fewer burns than was written in their medical records, because the cures he effected had all the earmarks of being close to marvelous. It took quite a long while, and numerous exceptional remedies before such work were generally understood and acknowledged.

Once in a while, the cynic and the patient are the same individuals. We need the results, but we battle to accept that it truly will work. At the conscious level, our minds are very much aware of the contrast between what we imagine and physical reality. In any case, another astounding hypnotic marvel shows that it doesn't make a difference what we accept at the conscious level since trance permits our mind to react to a reality that is independent of what we deliberately think. This phenomenon is classified as "trance logic."

Trance logic was first recognized 50 years ago by a renowned researcher of hypnotic named Dr. Martin Orne, who worked for a long time at the University of Pennsylvania. Dr. Orne directed various tests that demonstrated that in hypnotic, individuals could carry on as though two absolutely opposing facts were valid simultaneously. In one study, he hypnotized a few people so they couldn't see a seat he put directly before them. Then he requested that they walk straight ahead. The subjects all swerved around the seat.

Notwithstanding, when examined regarding the chair, they reported there was nothing there. They couldn't see

27

the seat. Some denied that they had swerved by any means. They accepted they were telling the truth when they said they couldn't see the seat, but at another level, their bodies realized it was there and moved to abstain from hitting it.

The test showed that hypnotic permits the mind to work at the same time on two separate levels, accepting two isolated, opposing things. There is a possibility of being hypnotized and have a hypnotic gastric band fitted but then to "distinguish" with your conscious mind that you don't have surgical scars, and you don't have a physical gastric band embedded. Trance logic implies that a part of your mind can trust one thing, and another part can accept the direct opposite, and your mind and body can continue working, accepting that two unique things are valid. So, you will be capable to consciously realize that you have not paid a huge amount of dollars for a surgical process, but then at the deepest level of unconscious command, your body accepts that you have a gastric band and will act in like manner. Subsequently, your stomach is conditioned to signal "feeling full" to your brain after only a couple of mouthfuls. So, you feel satisfied, and you get to lose more weight.

Visualization Is Easier Than You Think

The hypnotic we use to make your gastric band uses "visualization" and "influence loaded imager." Visualization is the creation of pictures in your mind. We would all be able to do it. It is an interesting part of the reasoning. For instance, think about your front door and ask yourself which side the lock is on. To address that question, you see an image in your mind's eye. It doesn't make a difference at all how reasonable or bright the image is, it is only how your mind works, and you see as much as you have to see. Influence loaded imagery is the psychological term for genuinely significant pictures. In this process, we utilize pictures in the eye of the mind with emotional importance.

Although hypnotic recommendations are incredible, they are dramatically upgraded by ground-breaking images when we are communicating directly to the body. For instance, you will be unable to accelerate your heart just by telling it to beat faster. Still, If you envision remaining on a railroad line and seeing a train surging towards you, your heart accelerates pretty quickly. Your body overreacts to clear, meaningful pictures.

That is the reason I will portray your operation in the trance segment. It doesn't make a difference whether you are listening intentionally, your conscious mind will hear all it needs to recreate the real band, in a similar way that a clear image of a moving toward train rushing towards your influences your pulse rate. You don't have to hold the pictures of the operational procedures in your conscious mind, because during an activity you are anesthetized and unconscious. Notwithstanding what you intentionally recollect, underneath the hypnotic anesthesia, your conscious mind uses this information and imagery to introduce your gastric band in the right spot.

The Power of Context

Contextual cues are another huge part of hypnotic suggestion. For instance, when I played out my hypnotic stage show, the setting of the theatre, the lights, the stage, and the desires of the crowd all improved the hypnotic marvels, whether or not the members were consciously mindful of it. The equivalent is valid with the gastric band. I outlined in the last part, the planning that surgeons require before the physical gastric band operation, and, significantly, you follow a similar preparatory procedure too.

Keep in mind, naturally slim individuals eat cheeseburgers and chocolate and French fries, they simply don't eat them to abundance, since they can perceive the signs that let them know, "You've had enough." obviously, with your hypnotic gastric band those signs will be exceptionally boisterous and clear, and you basically won't have the option to eat to such an extent. In any case, the extraordinary bit of leeway is that you will likewise feel totally fulfilled.

Both hypnosis and meditation do offer a deeply relaxing, calming, and an extremely beneficial state of mind, which plays a significant role in helping you to get through your day. Besides, hypnosis and meditation are the keys to unusual calmness and positivity as you start to address psychological, physical, and social issues.

The distinction between meditation and hypnosis is distorted because they are wrapped around the same state of mind, but they have different belief systems in their purest form. Hypnosis is a common natural state of mind whereby you tend to concentrate on a single thought, while meditation is a means that you use to enter into a hypnotic state.

Meditation is often characterized by relaxation and visualization, especially when you are trying to find tranquility, and reconnect with your personality, or seek guidance on an issue. Notably, this form of meditation has a pure purpose, structure, and it makes use of visualization, to help shape your life, which is referred to as self-hypnosis.

Combinations of the two states of relaxation both provide incredible results as they help to take control of your mind and perception. Meditation is effective as it helps to empty the mind and free it of all thoughts, while hypnosis goal in mind is to either help to overcome an obstacle, develop confidence, or help you to rediscover your potential. It does not matter if you practice meditation or hypnosis, so long as it is pleasant and it offers a positive experience, then it's great.

These two states of mind are very vital to you if you wish to lead a fulfilled and happier life.

How they work

Normally, your conscious mind usually makes you aware of your thought processes. So, you only tend to think about the situations that you are facing and make the right choice of words and actions to overcome those situations. Also, the subconscious mind is a huge aspect of your thoughts as it functions "behind the scenes" and works closely with the conscious mind.

For instance, if you're consciously trying to remember where you placed your keys, the subconscious mind accesses the information reservoir in your subconscious mind to help you to find exactly where you placed your keys. Also, the subconscious mind helps you to complete tasks that seem automatic, like breathing and constructing sentences.

Hypnosis and meditation are the most natural ways for you to be able to directly access your subconscious mind, enhance your thought process, and act as the brain behind every operation. The conscious mind is most active when you are awake because it helps to evaluate your thoughts and determines which ideas to put into action. They are responsible for processing the acquired information that the subconscious mind needs. On the contrary, the subconscious mind is the one in control whenever you fall asleep. At that moment, it renders the conscious mind ineffective for your thinking.

This subconscious state of mind allows you to be able to control the brain and gain access to your information reservoir, where you could change your perception about an impending task. Also, it allows you to become more creative as it induces your impulses and imagination. Hypnosis and meditation work together through many different mechanisms. These techniques include emotion, change in self-perspective, body awareness, and attention regulation.

These components are necessary for helping with all the various aspects of your life, and when combined together, the cumulative process thus leads to an enhanced self-regulation capacity. If you lack this capacity on a personal level, then it will cause psychological suffering and distress for you. So, practicing meditation plays a significant role in helping you to develop command over the mind, and makes you capable of controlling your thoughts, when you're done meditating.

The main aim of practicing hypnosis and meditation is to help control your thoughts and achieve the things that seem impossible to achieve through the conscious mind.

The best time for hypnosis and meditation

To succeed in these practices, you should create a routine that will help to keep you on track as you practice often. These practices are very similar to the things that require daily commitment as one of the obvious parts of achieving your results.

The more you hypnotize and meditate, the more you will be able to take charge of your body. Daily practices are recommended so that you will be able to choose the best time for you, depending on your work schedule and lifestyle. It's better to practice meditation and hypnosis when waking up, during the lunchtime break, or before you sleep.

Also, the practice is suitable to do during morning break or immediately after you finish working. No matter your preferences, you should ensure that the time you choose fits into your lifestyle.

There are different ways of learning meditation, but the most important thing in meditation is the ability to be able to imagine and think about the changes that you are expecting to get in your life. Therefore, it does not matter whether you can visualize it or not; you have to make it a routine so that you will be able to transform your conscious mind and address any complex issue.

Hypnosis and meditation greatly help to enhance your feelings and make it easy for you to deal with all psychological problems like anxiety, stress, and depression. Also, if you want to experience a drastic weight loss and be able to control your eating habits, then you should incorporate hypnosis and meditation into your plan and make it a regular practice. You can practice meditation at any time and anywhere, as long as you stay inactive, and you don't experience any interruptions.

It is worth knowing that your unconscious thoughts are purely shaped by your experiences, memories, and expectations. These aspects help to drive your conscious actions without you even realizing it. Your subconscious mind normally sets you up to fail; that's why it's difficult for you to be able to address your bad habits.

Hypnosis is critical in helping to update and alter those negative thoughts, thus making it possible for you to be able to critical conditions like chronic pain, substance abuse, and weight loss. When you begin to train your mind to think differently about setting goals and challenges, then you will be able to get rid of those thoughts that are making you to self-sabotage. Your mind will become suggestible when you're in a trance state, which will then enable you to be able to access and influence your powerful subconscious assumptions. So by following this guide, you will be able to take positive actions towards the changes that you have successfully set for yourself.

Hypnosis session for weight loss

So now you can relax and take this time to wind yourself down, and allow all those tensions to start flowing out and disappearing. So just bring to mind to remember that hypnosis is just self-hypnosis, as you're reading this book now, that this is not something that someone will be able to do for you. Because hypnosis is simply a state of deep relaxation, which successfully helps you to bypasses your own critical factors so that the suggestions that are beneficial to your true self will be readily received and accepted by your deeper unconscious mind.

After all, trance is an everyday natural calming experience, and you're entering into that experience easily and effortlessly. So start by asking yourself, if you've ever put yourself in a calm relaxing state before this moment, and if so, you can recall all those calm and relaxing states that you've previously experienced, whether it's via your favorite hobby, an activity, a journey or a holiday.

The most important thing to realize is that you should bring to your mind, relaxation, and protective magical thinking practices each day in your waking state because you know that the practice imprints it in your mind. And as time goes by, it becomes easier for you to be able to gain the benefits of these experiences, which helps to promote self-acceptance.

Once they become permanently fixed into your mind, you will experience some positive changes in your life, and they will become active by helping you to create positive changes in your life that are for your benefit, and they will lead you forward towards a real realization of those changes. And as you speak directly to the deeper inner part of the self that controls your eating habits and weight, you will realize that you have been eating more food than the food that your body wants or needs. And also, you will realize that your mind controls your eating habits.

Now just seeing all those levers that you can adjust, you can then choose which one to use because you know that you have the power over your weight and your eating habits. And also you know what you're eating. The exact time and amount that you choose to eat are totally controlled in this place, which is the deeper part of your authentic self.

This part of the body is not your stomach or your appetite, but it really controls your food, but it is your own mind, and you get to ask that aspect of yourself beginning today, to develop new habits for yourself. And set new positive goals for yourself because you are laying a mental foundation for yourself, who is now a cheerful, attractive, positive, and authentic you. The great importance to this new you and to your healthy, active, and attractive body is that you are eating less food, and you're happier.

The more you smile, and the more relaxed you are, the better you will look and the better you will feel. Also, you will be able to find satisfaction in eating less and pride yourself in knowing that each time you do so, you are rewarding your slimmer, healthier, and natural self. And you will know that the slimmer you are deep within you as you exercise, this new strength will grow. And as you eat healthily and sensibly, you will find yourself filling satisfied, and you will discover that the exercise makes it more reinforce and more natural towards your authentic identity.

Because it is like using and strengthening your muscles to become stronger and stronger, now eating sensibly becomes easier, easier, in a practical, and the positive way means that you are mentally asking your body the foods it needs, and then you are taking the time to listen to your own body quietly. And always check in with your body on the little food that your body needs from time to time, and you will be able to take time to integrate these ideas on a deeper level.

If you are listening to these and choosing to drift into a deeper sleep, you can just do so. Now just feeling good will allow your body to be able to drift down and go into a deeper and restful sleep. If you want to get up and continue with your activities, then you have to count from one to five, and when you reach five, you can then open your eyes and come back to the fully conscious reality.

And so on counting one, you should allow yourself to come back to full conscious reality with relaxation and ease. Then as you count two, come back slowly to your full conscious reality, and as you count three, take some nice deep relaxing breath. Moreover, as you count four, allow your eyes to open as if you've bathed them with fresh water, and now, as you count five, open your eyes completely and adjust yourself to your environment while getting ready to carry on with your day's activity.

Chapter 4: Strategies and Mind Exercises that Help Alongside Hypnotic Gastric Band

When we think of weight management, our minds often go to diet and exercise. What's more important than hitting the gym is exercising our brain? If we make sure that the most important organ in our body is taken care of, we can be certain that other healthy habits will soon follow. You can diet, exercise, and do everything else you need to lose weight, but if you continually distract, deflect, or flat out avoid your problems and root issues, you will never find true happiness. The happier you are and the more aware you can be of your mental health, the better it will be in the end, which will also lead to overall better quality of life.

Keep a Journal

Keeping a journey is a healthy habit for many people no matter what their goals, but it's important for someone that wants to lose weight as well. By writing down your different portion measurements and exercise habits, you can better ensure that you'll have a basis for evaluation. When this is done, you can predict future problems that might keep you from your goals by looking back on the days of recorded mistakes or slipups. You can see what kinds of schedules and structures aren't working so you can create better habits in the end. The more extensive your journaling, the better you'll be able to create your own research study of your weight-loss journey, meaning you can share your progress or use it as a structure for future diets.

Avoid the Scale

The biggest issue with weight-loss strugglers comes when they see the number on the scale. Someone that wants to lose ten pounds might get discouraged if they find they only lost nine. Sometimes, people might even have to gain weight before they end up losing a pound. By avoiding the scale altogether, certain failures and disappointments can be avoided as well.

Find a different way to track your progress. You can have monthly weigh-ins, but it shouldn't be something that should be checked once a day. Our weight fluctuates so much throughout our journey that it isn't worth stressing over on a daily basis. Any checking that happens more than once a day is also likely a bad habit; you're using it to distract yourself from a bigger issue.

The Calorie Myth

When many people diet, they focus too much on calories. They'll see that a certain snack pack only has a hundred calories, which means that it's good for you, right? Wrong. When we focus too much on how many calories are in something, we're failing to look at all the other factors that make up that product. Something with zero calories might include harmful chemicals or hidden substances that are bad for us. Something with a ton of calories might be avoided even though it has a large number of vitamins and necessary fiber.

Calories should still be considered, as the more calories you take in, the more you have to burn through exercise. They still shouldn't be a basis for what foods you decide to eat. If you focus too much on calories, you'll end up losing sight of other important issues. Remember that weight loss isn't about numbers. What's on the scale or on the nutrition package is important in making certain measurements, but they shouldn't be the definitive goals that you're creating on your weight-loss journey.

Talk About It

Keeping things in is never good. In fact, it can feel pretty awful. Those that are overweight might find themselves feeling embarrassed about their weight. Maybe they end up making excuses for themselves when they eat certain foods, verbalizing these reasons to others around them as a form of validation. "Oh, I'll just start my diet tomorrow," you might hear someone say as they sneak a few extra cupcakes from the dessert table. This kind of discussion can be counterintuitive. Instead, try talking about the issues and struggles you have rather than about the way you're going to make up for your problems later. You might find that you end up getting some great advice from a person that's going through a similar struggle.

Avoid telling people about your goal before you get on track, however. Talking about your feelings, emotions, and struggles is always a good thing. Sometimes it just takes saying a thing out loud for it to feel real. However, many individuals set themselves up for failure by sharing their goals too early. Those that post on social media about how they're going to lose weight are actually less likely to follow through with their goals. Stay silent with the majority at the beginning of your journey, confiding in just those you know you can rely on and trust.

Affirmations

Practicing affirmations is an important mindset strategy in weight loss. An affirmation is a type of positive reinforcement that helps in combating negative thoughts. Instead of telling yourself you're "no good" because you didn't follow through with a small goal, you should give yourself an affirmation such as "I am capable of continuing" to remind yourself of how powerful you really are. Below is a list of positive affirmations you should use in order to combat negative thoughts and improve overall encouragement:

1)   I can do this. I am capable of losing weight, and I have the ability to reach my goals.

2)   I am exercising every day and eating healthy as often as possible. I am actually doing what I should be doing in order to achieve my goals.

3)   If I can start my journey, I can finish it.

4)   I do not need processed foods to feel happy. I can feel the same joy from cooking a healthy meal.

5)   I have exercised before and can do it again. It is hard to start, but I know that once I do, I have what it takes to finish my exercise routine.

6)   I am healing myself. I have been through challenging times and deserve to feel happy.

7)   I am loved and am full of love.

8)   I am losing weight to be healthy.

9)   I am beautiful no matter what size. Skipping one day at the gym does not mean that I am not beautiful.

10)   I am eating healthy food full of nourishment. I can feel the positive change in my body, and I know that I only have more to look forward to.

Time Management

The most important part of a weight-loss journey is time management. This doesn't mean setting a quick goal and achieving it as fast as possible. It's all about using time properly and understanding how long it takes to actually do something. We set ridiculous goals for ourselves in the hopes that we'll achieve something great, but what ends up happening is, as the end-date approaches, we become overwhelmed and are set up for disappointment. We have to be realistic with our time goals and consider all factors when making different plans.

Practice Patience

Patience is hard to achieve. Anyone that wants to lose weight hopes that they can just jump on the scale after eating a salad and see the number drop by double digits. We have to accept before starting a weight-loss journey that this will never happen. We won't be able to just lose the weight overnight.

Sometimes, patience is hard to have when exercising. Many people find themselves getting bored on treadmills or other machines that require a repetitive activity for minutes at a time. Use different exercise methods that you find fun or entertaining, such as a dance class or going on an interesting trail run. If the gym is your only option, use the boring moments on machines as a way to meditate.

Clear your head, not thinking of how much weight you want to lose or what else you have to do to get there. Just practice counting or focusing on a quiet place you find peace in, such as a beach or a park. Visualize this in order to find a place of meditation. It'll take practice, but you'll soon find that you can zone out and work hard if you just focus.

There is No Rush

Weight loss takes time; we can't emphasize that enough. Some diets and exercises will help you lose weight quicker than others, but overall, you're going to have to put in a lot of time to lose weight. Remember not to feel too rushed throughout this journey. You have to be strict and consistent to actually see results, but there's no point in forcing yourself into ridiculous time constraints. If you cause yourself anxiety over certain dates, you might feel the need to stress-eat or go through dangerous dieting practices to get there.

Set Small Goals

Instead of looking at a wedding coming up in a couple of months as your goal for losing weight, instead, use that as a small milestone. Many of us get worried about looking at the future, thinking of things coming up as the time limits for which we have to lose weight. Maybe it's March, and you only have a couple of months until the swimsuit season. Instead of going on a diet to lose thirty pounds in three months, use the beginning of summer as a small milestone in your journey. Aim, instead, to be healthier and more confident by the time summer comes, rather than giving yourself a ridiculous goal that you don't even know if you can achieve.

Many people have an unhealthy perception of dieting when looking at certain periods of time. Maybe it's a Tuesday, and so they tell themselves that next Monday is going to be the date to start dieting. In preparation for that date, that same person might make sure to eat all the junk in their house to make sure temptation is removed. But then, by the time Monday comes, something else happens that delays it further.

Even worse, maybe it's Sunday night, and you decide that since tomorrow is Monday, you're going to start your diet right now. But then, Tuesday comes, and the diet doesn't start, so you feel discouraged, and you count that as just another time that you failed! Don't do this! Instead, set a starting point much further into the future. Find a date two weeks away, whether it's on a Monday, the first of the month, or just a random Wednesday. That way, you can prepare for the official diet-start date. This way, you can practice as the actual date approaches.

For example, your New Year's resolution might be to lose weight. If that's the case, throughout December, you should practice incorporating workout routines a few times a week and experiment with healthy dinners. Then, when January comes around, you have more experience in dieting and are better prepared to actually start your journey than if you had only given yourself a few days to prep.

Something to Tend

Your weight is something to tend. Think of it as a plant. You don't just plant a flower and walk away. The flower will grow, but if you don't go back and make sure to water it, the flower will die. Your journey is a flower. By purchasing this book, you've purchased the seeds. As you read these words, you're reading how to plant the seed and how to make sure that it stays alive. After you've finished the book, it's time to plant the seed. This is done by creating a workout plan and diet.

Once the flower blossoms, you'll have reached your weight-loss goal. Just like the flower, if you abandon your goals and don't tend to your weight-loss journey, you will fall off track and go back into your old lifestyle.

You must read and use this part before you fit your hypnotic gastric band. You have to change your mental self-image, your conduct, and your emotions to appreciate and profit by your new slim body completely. If you don't set yourself up, there is an opportunity you could feel awkward or befuddled and neglect to appreciate the advantages of losing weight permanently. This section will guide you on how to lose more weight, you will feel more joyful and confident, and you will have every one of the instruments you have to manage the new circumstances that emerge. When your hypnotic gastric band is fitted, your life will change. You will eat less and get slimmer; however, you will likewise encounter a course of changes that will influence every part of your life. You will also be taking part in a considerably greater change that is moving through society. You will be a part of the movement away from diets towards a genuine healthy weight loss procedure. Starting now, you will eat unexpectedly; however, you won't diet, because diets don't work.

Diets Don't Work

Dieting makes the body thinks the individual is starving, so the more they diet, the more they wind up bingeing. When they arrive at their target weight, their body feels it has been starving for a long time, so when they loosen up, it retaliates and gets them to go straight into an unhealthy pattern of overeating. The scientific research is clear and undeniable. Most of the dieters get slimmer temporarily, and after a while, get the weight back on. More regrettable still, more than 70 percent end up heavier than when they began dieting. It is no big surprise that there is presently an army of doctors who are moving against the diet business and diet clubs because, for more than 90 percent of individuals, diets don't work! The diet business insiders have known this dreary truth for quite a long time, but still, they sell their money-making schemes. What's more, even though the proof of disappointment is surrounding us, individuals continue unveiling diet plans daily.

Guilt

One of the reasons numerous overweight individuals battle endlessly with diets is guilt. At some level, they accept their excess weight is their own shortcoming. They feel regretful, so they think they merit the suffering of denying themselves food and delight from food. These individuals begin feeling awful, and then because dieting doesn't work, they feel much more dreadful. I absolutely don't believe anybody is a terrible individual because the person is overweight. If you are overweight, it isn't your flaw, and it is the deficiency of your body's programming. You have had bad programming introduced that has just unbalanced the natural system of delight and sustenance from food. I totally realize that you can get slimmer and feel better and appreciate the process.

Gambling

Another explanation that a large number of individuals go on diets, again and again, is the law of intermittent reinforcement. This is a similar motivation behind why individuals become dependent on gambling. The truth of the matter is that even though in the long run, a gambler consistently loses, he does occasionally win. In any case, he never knows precisely when he will win. The likelihood that this time he may win keeps him betting "one more time." This is the intermittent reinforcement. It is the same with diets. Practically all individuals lose more weight in the first month of a diet, and they continue trusting that on this diet, the weight loss will proceed. And, just every so often, incidentally, it does. We, as a whole, know at any rate a couple of individuals who have figured out how to lose more weight regardless of the considerable number of issues of diets. Dieters will, in general, take a look at them—the less than One 0 percent who are fruitful—rather than the 90 percent who come up short. I don't believe in gambling. I believe in a rational, logical way to deal with life. My way of dealing with weight loss and my hypnotic gastric band depends on the best accessible proof to date. Seven out of ten individuals who use my weight loss system get in shape and keep it off. The hypnotic gastric band builds that success rate to more than nine out of ten.

Diet Promotion

Anybody would think that it's simpler to remain on a diet if they had a group of individuals controlling their food consumption. Diet clubs likewise search out a specific sort of specialist, somebody who is set up to support them and consequently be very generously compensated. I was drawn nearer by these diet clubs years ago when I began faulting them, to check whether we could "cooperate." Well, I double-checked the exploration then, and I affirmed the realities. When individuals use my system appropriately over a long time, it works. When individuals diet over a long time, it doesn't work. I could perceive any reason why they needed me to underwrite their items, but there was nothing in it for you or for me. It would have been unscrupulous.

In the years later, I have always asked diet clubs to go along with me on a broadcast discussion to discuss the benefits and achievements of our various ways to deal with weight loss. In each one of those years, they have never figured out how to take up my call, disregarding all the free exposure it speaks to. Amusingly, diet clubs are not in the weight-loss business.

They do make camaraderie with their weekly gatherings, and that is really an excellent thing since it is extraordinary to have support when you are on a mission. In any case, the gatherings are not their genuine source of benefit. They are an approach to keep individuals included and near their items. As individuals become less effective at getting in shape through willpower alone, they become progressively defenseless to purchasing items that guarantee wonders. What's more, the diet clubs make their genuine money selling low-fat, chemically altered food, and food substitutes. They are in the artificial food business.

Hostile

Some individuals have asked me for what valid reason I am so unfriendly to the diet business. Why don't I simply quiet down and acknowledge that various individuals have various ways to deal with weight loss? The appropriate response is that I feel very strongly about the subject. I feel irate in the interest of the considerable number of individuals I have met in my weight loss workshops who have languished over the years using diets that caused them to feel guilt and disappointment, and still left them overweight. If diets simply didn't work, that would be terrible enough. However, the reality they leave such a large number of individuals significantly heavier than before they began that gets me truly worked up. I believe this is the principal reason behind why we currently have 60 percent of individuals in the U.K. also, the U.S. overweight is many years of dieting. Diets and diet clubs are the issue!

If we take a look at the science of hypnotic gastric band and weight loss, you need to check on your dieting. Diets and diet clubs are causing enormous measures of hopelessness and ill health, putting an immense weight on our country's social insurance system. Starving your body gives you the fake idea that the diet is working, while you are losing muscle mass, not fat (absolutely an inappropriate sort of weight), and simultaneously slowing metabolism. It is simple waye killing you, they know it, and everything they can consider is benefits! When I see somebody overweight, I don't simply observe layers of fat. I see layers of dissatisfaction, brought about by a gathering of critical money-makers who couldn't care less for the individuals they misuse, nor about the harm they are causing to the lives of the individuals they should help. So when the diet clubs take my mottos when discussing weight loss, it just makes me increasingly resolved to uncover them and show whatever number individuals as could be allowed that it is so natural to get in shape.

Quit Worrying about Food

I have gone on about diets for two reasons. One, as should be obvious, is that I am enthusiastic about the theme. Secondly, if you have ever dieted earlier, you are currently going to alter your dietary patterns radically. Your hypnotic gastric band will assist you with getting in shape, and you will currently need to eat contrastingly, so you make the most of your new body and don't undermine your bliss with the propensities for dieting. Dieters stress over food. They naturally isolate food into "good" and "bad."

On diets, they consider food practically constantly—except for when they are eating, when they jolt their food and feel regretful You are not dieting, so you can quit stressing. You won't gorge, so you can get hungry, eat appropriately, and truly appreciate it. Try not to starve yourself. Those days are long gone. You never again must be scared of food. You can quit pondering on it when you are not eating. Now, you can get hungry the normal way and eat appropriately. That implies you truly feel the body's natural want for food and truly fulfill everything securely ensured by your hypnotic gastric band.

A short time ago, I was on TV discussing food, and a lady called in and stated, "I need to thank you for helping me escape from food prison." I asked her what she implied by that. She clarified, "I used to count calories, I weighed myself consistently, and I pondered about food continually. Your system has helped me to understand that my weight naturally goes here and there a bit, I don't need to get frenzy, and I don't need to diet. I'm slimmer than I at any point was, and I make the most of my food ." She had discovered that having a thin, healthy body isn't an ordeal. It is a natural, fulfilling lifestyle.

Life Changes

When you get in shape, your whole life changes. Since you have a hypnotic gastric band, you won't have the option to gorge, so you must set yourself up for every one of the progressions that are coming in your direction. Indeed, even the best things on the planet bring challenges, and we have to figure out how to deal with them, and your prosperity will have exceptionally huge results. For instance, it is anything but difficult to think, "Gracious, I wish I could live in a major, extravagant house," and surely, it would be pleasant to have all the space. Be that as it may, you'll additionally need to figure out what to look like after it! If you would prefer not to invest all your energy cleaning it, you'll need to figure out how to use the ideal individuals and how to deal with making them work surrounding you.

You likewise would need to manage some different things that you probably won't consider from the outset, for example, the various ways individuals treat you and your property when you live in a noteworthy house. It isn't in every case simple—the papers have customary tales about lottery victors who experience difficulties adapting to all that their money has brought them. That correlation isn't extreme. Actually, getting slimmer will transform yourself in a far more profound and more positive route than winning a huge amount of money or exchanging up to a multimillion-dollar house.

Chapter 6: Weight Loss by Stopping Emotional Eating

Emotional eating normally occurs when your food becomes a tool that you use in responding to any internal or external emotional cues. It's normal for human beings to tend to respond to any stressful situation and the difficult feelings that they have. Whenever you have stressful emotions, you tend to run after a bag of chips or bars of chocolate, a large pizza, or a jar of ice cream to distract yourself from that emotional pain. The foods that you crave at that moment are referred to as comfort food. Those foods contain a high calorie or high carbohydrate with no nutritional value.

Do you know that your appetite increases whenever you are stressed, and whenever you're stressed, you tend to make poor eating habits? Stress is associated with weight gain and weight loss. When you are under intense stress and intense emotions like boredom or sadness, you tend to cleave unto food. Now that's emotion napping, and it is the way that your body relieves itself of the stress and gets the energy that it needs to overcome its over-dependence on food. Normally get you to the point whereby you don't eat healthy anymore.

Emotional eating is a chronic issue that affects every gender, both male and female, but research have shown that women are more prone to emotional eating than men. Emotional eaters tend to incline towards salty, sweet, fatty, and generally high-calorie foods. Normally these foods are not healthy for the body, and even if you choose to eat them, you should only eat them with moderation. Emotional eating, especially indulging in unhealthy food, end up affecting your weight.

Emotional eating was defined as eating in response to intense emotional emotions. Many studies reveal that having a positive mood can reduce your food intake, so you need to start accepting the fact that positive emotions are now part of emotional eating in the same way that negative emotions are part of emotional eating.

Effects of Emotional Eating

So here are some effects of emotional eating.

Intense Nausea

 When you are food binging, the food provides a short-term distraction to the emotions that you are facing, and more than often, you will tend to eat very quickly, and as a result, you will overeat. This will then result to stomach pains or nausea, and this can last for one or two days. So it is very important to concentrate on the problem, that is causing you stress, instead of eating food to solve that problem.

Feeling Guilty

The next one is feeling guilty. Occasionally, you may use food as a reward to celebrate something that is not necessarily bad. It is very important to celebrate the little wings that you have in life, and if food is the way you choose to celebrate it, then you should choose to eat healthy meals instead of going for unhealthy meals. However, when food becomes your primary mechanism for coping with emotional stress whenever you feel stressed, upset, lonely, angry or exhausted, then you will open the fridge and find yourself in an unhealthy cycle, without even being able to target to the root cause of the problem that is making you stressed.

Furthermore, you will be filled with guilt. Even after all the emotional damage has passed away, you will still be filled with remorse for what you have done and for the unhealthy lifestyle that you choose to make at that moment, which will then lower your self-esteem. And then, you will go into another emotional eating outburst.

Weight-Related Health Issues

The next one is weight-related health issues. I'm sure that you are aware of how unhealthy eating affects your weight. Many researchers have discovered that emotional eating affects the weight both positively and negatively. Generally, the foods that you crave during those emotional moments are foods that are high in sugar, high in salt and saturated fats. And in those emotional moments, you tend to eat anything that you can lay your hands on.

Now even though some healthy fast foods are available out there, many of them are still filled with salt, sugar, and trans fat content. High carbohydrate food increases the demand for insulin in the body, which then promotes hunger more and more, and therefore you tend to eat more calories than you are supposed to consume. Consuming a high level of fat can have an immediate impact on your blood vessels, and it does that in the short-term. In the end, if you consume too much fat, your blood pressure will increase, and you will become hospitable to heart attack, kidney disease, and another cardiovascular disease. Many manufactured fats are created during food processing, and those fat are fats that are found in pizza, dough, crackers, fried pies, cookies, and pastries.

Do not be misinformed; no amount of saturated fat is healthy. If you continue to eat this kind of food, you'll be putting yourself in the risks of HDL and LDL, which is the good kind of cholesterol and the bad kind of cholesterol. And to be frank, both of them will put your heart into the risk of diabetes, high cholesterol, obesity, high blood pressure, and insulin resistance. So these are some of the challenges that you will face when you engage in emotional eating outbursts.

How to stop emotional eating using Meditation

Right now, you already know what to eat, and you already know what not to eat, and you already know what is good for your body and what is not good for your body. Now even if you're not a nutritionist or a health coach or a fitness activist, you already know these things. But when you are alone, you tend to engage in emotional eating, and you successfully keep it to yourself and make sure that no one knows about it. It is just like you surrender your control for food to a food demon, and when that demon possesses you, you become angry, sad and stress at once and before you know what is happening, you have gone to your fridge, opened it and begin to consume whatever is there.

As strong as you, once this food demon has possessed you, it will convince you that food is the only way to get out of that emotional turmoil that you are facing. So before you know what is happening, you are invading your refrigerator and consuming that jar of almond butter that you promised yourself not to consume. And just a few seconds that you open the jar of almond butter, you take the bottle and put it in your mouth, and when you close the door again. And you do it again and again and again, and before you know what is happening, you have leveled

57

the jar up to halfway, and not a dent has been made on the initial in motion that you were eating over.

Now before you know it, if your consciousness catches up with you. You start to feel sad, guilt, and shame. The almond butter that you were eating didn't help you that much, not in the way that you wanted it to help you. So if there is anything that you need to realize is that you now feel worse than you were one hour ago. And so you make a promise that you won't repeat this again and that this is the last time that this will happen.

You promised yourself never to share an entrance with that almond butter again, but then you realize that this is what you have been doing to the gluten-free cookies, to that ice cream, and hot chocolate before now. If this is your behavior, then you'll be able to relate to this. Emotional eating is a strong addition that you must stop. It is more of a habit and one not easy to control. So there is hope for you if you are engaging in emotional eating today. You have to be able to have control by yourself and over your emotional eating. So there are many strategies that you can use to combat that emotional eating, and one of them is meditation.

Now when it comes to emotional eating and weight management, it is important to acknowledge the connection between our minds and our bodies. Today we live in a very busy and packed world that is weighing us down. However, mindful meditation can be a powerful tool to help you to be able to create a rational relationship with the food that you eat. One of the most important things about overcoming emotional eating is not to avoid the emotions, but rather to face them head-on and to accept them the way they are and to accept that they are a crucial part of your life.

If you want to put a stop to emotional eating, then you need to be able to shift your beliefs and your worthiness. You need to be able to create a means to cope with unhealthy situations. It is very important to note that meditation will not cure your emotional eating completely. Rather it will help you to examine and rationalize all the underlining sensations that are leading to emotional eating in your life. For emotional eaters, the feeling of guilt, shame, and low self-esteem are very common.

Frequently these negative create judgment in their mind and triggers unhealthy eating patterns, and they end up feeling like an endless self-perpetuating loop. Meditation helps you to be able to develop a non-judgmental mindset about observing your reality. And that mindset will be able to help with you and suppress your emotions negative feelings, without even trying to suppress them or comfort them with foods.

Develop the Mind, and Body connection

Meditation will help you to develop the mind and body connection. And once you're able to develop that connection, you will be able to distinguish between emotional eating and physical hunger, and once you can distinguish between that, you'll be able to recognize your cues for hunger and safety. You will instantly tell when your hunger is not related to physical hunger. Research indicates that medication will help to strengthen your prefrontal cortex, which is the part of the brain that helps you with will power. That part of the brain is the part of the brain that allows us to resist the urge is within us.

Mindfulness will help the urges to eat even when they're not hungry.

By strengthening that prefrontal cortex, you'll be able to get comfortable at observing those impulses without acting on them. If you want to get rid of an unhealthy habit and start to build new ones, then you need to be able to work on your prefrontal cortex, and you can only do that with meditation. Once you start meditating, you will start reaping the benefits. You will learn how to be able to live more in the present. You'll become more aware of your thinking patterns, and in no time, you will be able to become conscious of how you treat food. You'll be able to make the right choice when it comes to food.

Meditation is in fashion. As soon as you tell someone that you have a problem, it is a rare occasion when they do not recommend you to practice it. It doesn't matter if the problem is mental or physical.

Sometimes, people's insistence leads us to reject a plan idea. However, wouldn't it be more interesting to ask why so many people agree to advise you the same thing?

Interest in Eastern cultures brought the influence of ideas to the forefront. And they're our existence's nucleus. Nutrition and physical exercise promote our body's optimal working.

Yet it's also true that when our emotions aren't controlled, the brain secretes substances that affect our body and mind.

Therefore, physical sufferings or thoughts that make life difficult for us can appear. In this way, meditation helps to keep us safe.

Practicing anti-stress meditation at home

We know that sometimes it costs. How to combine our daily obligations with that moment of anti-stress meditation? We get up with things to do and arrive at bed with a mind full of those tasks and commitments that must be fulfilled for the next day.

Be careful if the previous paragraph is an example of what you always live in your day today. It is essential that you know how to organize times and set limits, control all those pressures that do not allow you to get rest.

Ideally, you learn to balance your life. Where you are always the priority of taking care of your health and your emotions. Stress can hurt you a lot, and you should see it as an enemy to dominate, to do small to be able to handle it properly. We explain how to practice anti-stress meditation.

1. Emotional agenda

Do you keep an agenda in your day to day of the things you should do? Of your obligations, appointments, meetings, appointments with teachers of children, or your visit to the doctor?

Do the same with your emotions, with your personal needs. Spend at least one hour or two hours for yourself each day. To do what you like, to be alone, and to practice anti-stress meditation. Your emotions have priority, make a hole in your day today. You deserve it, and you need it.

2. A moment of tranquility

It doesn't matter where it is. In your room, in the kitchen or in a park. You must be calm and surrounded by an environment that is pleasant, placid, and comforting. If you want, put on the music that you like, but you must be alone.

3. Regulate your breathing

Let's now take care of our breathing. Once you are comfortable, start to take a deep breath through your nose. Allow your chest to swell, then let this air out little by little through your mouth. If you repeat it six or seven times, you will begin to notice a comforting tingling through your body, and you feel better and calmer.

4. Focus thoughts

What will we do next? Visualize those pressures that concern you most. Are you pressured at work? Do you have problems with your partner? Visualize those images and keep breathing. The tension should soften, the nerves should lose their intensity, and the fear will soften. You will feel better little by little.

5. Positive images

Once you have focused those images, what more pressure they cause on your being, let's now go on to visualize pleasant things, aspects that you would like to be living, and that would make you happy.

They must be simple things: a walk on the beach, you touching the bark of a tree, you walk through a quiet city where the sun illuminates your face and where the rumor of nearby coffee shops envelops you with a pleasant smell of coffee ... Easy things, make you happy. Visualize it and keep breathing deeply.

6. The silence

Now we close our eyes. At least for two minutes. Try not to think about anything; just let the silence envelop you. You are at peace, and you are well, there is no pressure. There are only you and a quiet world where there are no pressures and threats, and everything is warm and pleasant.

7. Open your eyes in a renewed way

It is time to open your eyes and breathe normally again. Look around without moving, without getting up. Don't do it, or you'll run the risk of getting dizzy. Allow about five minutes to pass before you walk again. Surely you feel much better, lighter, and without any pressure on your body.

8. New perspectives

Now that you feel more relaxed, try to think about what you can do to find yourself better day by day. Being a little happier sometimes requires that we have to make small changes. And the good thing about anti-stress meditation is that it is slowly changing us inside.

It requires us to make small changes to find the balance so that the body and the mind feel in tune again, and the pressures, the anxieties go out of our body like the smoke that escapes through a window.

Meditation for a Deep and Quick Sleep

Sleep is incredibly important, but sometimes falling asleep can be difficult if we are not in the right mindset.

For this activity, we are going to take you through a visualization that will help ensure that you can get a deep sleep. It's important before falling asleep to relax your mind so that you can travel gently throughout your brain.

Start off by noticing your breath. Breathe in through your nose and out through your mouth. This is going to help calm you down so that you are able to breathe easier.

Begin by breathing in for five and out for five as we count down from twenty. Once we reach one, your mind will be completely clear. Each time a thought passes in, you will think of nothing. You will have nothing in your sight, and you will only think with your mind.

Make sure that you are in a comfortable place where you can sink into the space around you. Let your body become heavy as it falls into the bed. Keep your eyes closed and see nothing in front of you but darkness.

Remember to breathe in for five and out for five. Keep an empty mind and be ready to travel through a journey that will take you to a restful place.

Count from 20 down to 1

You see nothing in front of you, it is completely dark, and you feel your body lifting gently up like a feather. You are light against the bed, and nothing is keeping you down. Continue to feel your body rise higher and higher. You are floating in space. There's black nothingness around you. You are gently drifting around.

You can see a few stars dotting the sky so far away, but for the most part, you see nothing. You feel yourself slowly moving through space. Your body is light and free, and nothing is keeping you strapped down. You're not afraid in this moment.

You are simply feeling easy and free. Breathe in and out, in and out.

You start to drift more towards a few planets, throughout your journey in space. You can really see now that you are up in the highest parts of the galaxy. You see out of the corner of your eye that you can actually catch a glimpse of Earth. You start gently floating towards it, having to put no effort in at all as your body is like a space rock floating through the stars.

Nothing is holding you down.

Nothing is violently pushing you either. Everything that you feel is a gentle and free emotion. You get closer and closer to Earth now and can see all the clouds that surround you. You start to move down, and you gently enter into the cloud area. Normally gravity would pull you down so fast, but right now you're just simply a gentle body drifting through the air. You get closer and closer to the land. You can see some birds here and there and a few cars and lights on the ground beneath you.

You pass all of this, gently floating over a sleepy town.

Look down and let your mind explore what it is that you see down there. What is it that is in front of your eyes? What do you notice about this world around you as you continue to go closer and closer to home?

You are gently drifting throughout the sky. You can see trees beneath you. Now, if you reached your hand down, you'd even be able to gently feel a few leaves on the tops of the tallest trees. You don't do this now because you're just concerned with continuing to float through the sky. That's all that you really care about in this moment.

You're getting closer and closer and closer to home now, almost ready to fall asleep. You start to see that there is a lake.

You gently float down to the surface of the lake, and you land right in a boat. Your body is a little bit heavier now. You feel it relax into the bottom of the boat. Nothing around you concerns you right now. You feel no stress or tension in any part of your body. You are simply floating through this space now.

The boat starts to drift on the lake gently. It is dark out now, and you look up and see all the stars in the sky. All of this reminds you of the place that you were just a few moments ago. You start to drift closer and closer to sleep.

Do you feel as the tension leaves your body? You are peaceful throughout. You are not holding on to anything that causes you stress or anxiety. You are at ease in this moment. Everything feels good, and you have no fear. You drift around in the water now for a little bit longer. You can see everything so clearly in this night sky. Just because it is dark does not mean that it's hard to see. The moon casts a beautiful glow over everything around you. You can feel the moon charging your skin. As you drift closer and closer to sleep, you feel almost nothing in your body now. You continue to focus on your breathing. You are safe, and you are at peace. You are calm, and you are relaxed. You feel incredible in this moment.

The boat starts to lift from the water. You feel as it gets higher above the water. You are even heavier now. Now you are completely glued to this comfortable surface as the boat starts to fly through the sky. You can look down and see that the city beneath you has drifted to sleep. You're getting closer and closer to home now. You can actually see your home beneath you. The boat gently takes you to your front door, and you float right in. No need to walk or climb stairs. You simply float in and straight to your bed.

You fall delicately into your bed with your head resting nicely on a pillow.

Here you are, in this moment, so peaceful and so relaxed. You are completely at ease. There's nothing that stresses you out or causes any anxiety or tension now. You are simply a body that is trying to fall asleep.

As we count down from 20, you will drift off to sleep. You will be in a very relaxed state where nothing stresses you out. You're not concerned with things that happened in the past, and you aren't going to stay up in fear of what might happen tomorrow, you are asleep. You are relaxed.

Breathe in and out. Breathe in and out.

Count down from 20 to 1

Sometimes we allow ourselves to fill every hole in our belly, and typically we have many different excuses for doing so. From classical excuses such as "I will start my diet tomorrow" all the way to "just one more bite." Whatever excuse we have, it is just our own permission to feel bad in the future about our weight and the way we look. The most common reason why we come up with any excuse is that we are trying to increase our sense of comfort. And that is perfectly fine if you want to increase your sense of comfort, but choose the strategy that will not make you feel bad about yourself in the future.

Listening to this guided hypnosis is a good strategy to limit your food intake with the power of your mind, so you can stop binge eating, and certainly start feeling the benefits of sticking to a healthier lifestyle.

We will begin this guided hypnosis session by becoming consciously aware that we are always in control and always have a choice. At this moment, the only choice you need to make now is to choose to go into a deep relaxation right now...or in a few moments...when you make yourself more comfortable...at ease...and when you tell yourself..."I am going to relax...now...completely and effortlessly...while my subconscious mind learns everything that is needed to stop my binge eating..."

Start inhaling purposefully, and a bit deeper than usual... then slowly push all the air out as much as you can...and once you push all the air out pause for a second before you start inhaling again...

One more time...take another deep breath in, and purposefully and slowly push all the air out completely...and once all the air is out...pause for a second before you start inhaling again...that is right...just like that...and don't be surprised if you can already notice that the old compulsions are just starting to melt away...very slowly...as you inhale deeply and allow yourself to relax...

Continue breathing at a steady pace...just like you normally do...and allow the air moving in and out of your lungs and belly to deepen your relaxation...

Imagine that each time you inhale...relaxation energy fills your head, neck, and chest...and as you exhale, that relaxation energy spreads through the rest of your body...just like a wave...

Filling your head, neck, and chest and as you inhale...and spreading that relaxation energy all over your body as it goes down...your arms and belly...all the way down your legs and feet...washing away your worries, concerns and troubling thoughts...

Continue your relaxation by releasing everyday worries, concerns, and troubling thoughts...by simply directing your focus to your body. Make yourself comfortable before you get completely absorbed by the sound of my voice that will lead you into a perfect state of mind to let go...release...and free yourself completely from binge eating...and become more determined to limit your food intake...

As you make those final small adjustments...I would like you to mentally become aware of your feet...it doesn't matter if you are sitting or lying down...as long as you are aware of the sensation in your feet right now...

At this moment, become aware of the sensation in your feet...and imagine how light they would feel like, just after one week of stopping binge eating and consciously limiting your food intake...

Instruct all the small muscles in your feet to relax...and as your feet become even more relaxed...allow that relaxation to slowly move upwards...up your calves and knees...making your muscles soft...and lose...completely relaxed...

Fill that relaxation in your thighs...making you experience that pleasant heaviness of completely relaxed muscles in your legs...

Relaxation and that inspiring image of limiting your food intake are moving up your torso...lower back...and wraps itself gently around your stomach...and slowly start shrinking your stomach to a size that can match your consciously determined limit of food intake as you are becoming even more relaxed...

Each time you think of food and eating, you see this image wrapping around your stomach tightly so it allows only a limited amount of food that is enough for you to stay healthy and become fit...

And naturally, as relaxation reaches your chest, you feel a strong desire to inhale deeply...and fill your lungs with air...as your upper body evenly distributes that relaxation across your shoulders and arm all the way to your fingertips...and that tingling sensation that you feel in your fingers and palms are there only to remind you that you are about to go into a wonderfully relaxed state of mind...perfect for you to completely let go of all the worries, concerns and stop binge eating...but not just yet...there is no rush...you will do this soon...

Before you go into a wonderfully relaxed state of mind, I would like you to imagine that you are standing in front of a staircase that is leading up... You can see ten steps in front of you...and as I count from one to ten, you will imagine that you are climbing those stairs...and with each and new step, your decision to limit your food intake becomes stronger...the moment you hear me say "ten" you will naturally go into a wonderfully relaxed state of mind and body...and find your self in a room with a dining table and a chair...

Starting to climb the stairs...one...two...feeling that familiar sense of determination ...three...four...increasing the willpower behind your intention to limit your food intake...five...six...feeling deeply satisfied with the decision to stop binge eating...seven...eight...choosing only to have 20 bites of fresh and healthier food for each meal...nine...TEN...you are now at the top of the staircases in a room with a dining table...feeling completely relaxed and with a strong determination to limit your food intake to 20 bites per meal...

This will happen on its own...you don't have to do anything...yet...your body and your subconscious mind will know how to do that for you...once you are ready to let go...release...and free yourself completely...so that you can make more space for building a more stronger intention and follow through your decision to limit your food intake and choose food that is beneficial for your well being...

Consciously imagine a big green number twenty...and see it in your mind... Imagine that this is the number of bites that you are taking per each meal that you have... These twenty bites of carefully chosen healthier food are the perfect amount for the new size of your stomach...that is wrapped up in that inviting image and the idea of limiting your food intake...and stopping binge eating for good...

Each meal you are about to start, remember that big green number twenty...and you instantly know that you have the opportunity to enjoy this healthy food meal as you make your determination to have an healthier lifestyle even stronger...

Give clear instructions to your subconscious mind to follow your lead and assist you in creating this habit and choices by visualizing yourself doing this...Visualize that you are sitting at the table covered with all kinds of food...and even though that everything is available you are deciding to choose only healthy food that is good for your well being...and you are also deciding to have just a limited amount of that food...

As you prepare yourself to start eating, a big green number twenty appears in front of you...to remind you to completely enjoy these twenty bites of delicious healthy food...

You take the first bite...and start chewing very slowly...so you can experience all the flavors...and satisfy your senses...

Nineteen....you take another bite and you notice the fresh smells of your food as you chew slowly...

Eighteen...you are becoming more mindful when you are eating...and you can notice all the soft sound you make as you are slowly chewing your healthy food...

Seventeen...you are now aware of all the movements that your mouth, tongue, and jaw are making while you are eating...

Sixteen...your awareness is following your food from the moment it touches your mouth, as it makes it way over the tongue...down your throat...into your stomach...

Fifteen...your subconscious mind learns everything that is needed that will stop your binge eating disorder...

You continue to eat slowly...and mindfully as you enjoy every bite...you are now at number ten, and you can notice that your stomach is becoming full... A few more delicious bites and you are now at the number five...nearly there...but far away from old habits...so far away from old compulsions...far away from binge eating...

Now you have one more bite to complete your conscious food intake limit...and when you eat this last bite you feel that your stomach is completely full...and you feel very good about yourself...you know that this is the right choice for you to accomplish your diet goals...

The delicious and healthy meal is now finished...you stand up and move away from the table...and as you are starting to make your way back to that staircase, the first thing you are starting to notice is that you are lighter and that your feet really relaxed and lighter than before...so proud of your self, because you are doing it...you are finally taking control...

In a moment I will ask you to start going down the stairs as I count down from ten to one...and the moment you hear me say "one" you will allow your subconscious mind to take this vision of you happily enjoying twenty bites for each meal and make it into a new habit...

You will continue to do so, naturally and effortlessly until you are satisfied with the choices you are making to live a new and healthier way of life...or until you find another strategy or a new behavior that will work even better than this for you to stop binge eating and achieve your diet goals...

Start going down the stairs as I do the countdown...ten...nine...filing your subconscious mind with all the necessary information that it needs to support you in this important journey...eight...seven...thinking about all the benefits that will come with your healthy lifestyle...six...five...your decision to limit your food intake is getting stronger...and stronger...four...three...you are following through your plan...two...you take only twenty bites per meal...one...allowing your subconscious mind to create all the changes required to support your new habit...and your healthy lifestyle...

You are now at the bottom of the stairs...and you can see yourself integrating all of these learnings and useful insights...as you prepare yourself to slowly come back to this present moment in time...and whenever you are ready...open your eyes and become fully awake and aware of your strong decision to make healthy choices.

Chapter 9: The Satisfaction Factor

Wise Japanese people consider pleasure an important aspect of a good lifestyle. In the fierce pursuit of thinness and health, we often overlook one of the main gifts of life - the pleasure and satisfaction of the process of absorption of food. When you eat what you really want in a welcoming environment, the pleasure you receive becomes a powerful help in achieving satisfaction and comfort. Try it yourself and find that to feel "enough" you will need to eat much less.

So what's so satisfying that gives him such power? According to the teachings of Abraham Maslow, we are driven by unfulfilled needs. We want what we can't get, and we are ready to do anything to calm down the feeling of deprivation that inevitably arises when our needs are not realized. Dissatisfaction - whether in food, relationships, or careers - makes us unhappy.

To bring pleasure, your meal should consist of dishes that you like and "hit the bull's eye." Choking on the salad, when you want fried meat, you will not reach satisfaction. If you are offered a delicious meal or a whole meal when you are not very hungry, joy is reduced. You may still eat, but with moderate hunger, the food is much tastier. On the contrary, if you eat when you are very hungry, the taste buds hardly have time to notice the refined taste of the dishes before you swallow the whole dinner. What satisfaction is there! But when you start a tasty dish with a moderate feeling of hunger, then, most likely, before the end of the meal, you will feel that you are full. If you finish off the whole lunch at once, the taste of food will be weakened. Taste papillae lose sensitivity to food shades, especially when overeating.

Imagine a quarrel with a family member in the midst of, for example, dinner. Do you like to eat in such an environment? Yes, you may not notice what you ate! Or think about how you felt when you ate in the hope of crushing emotions. Again, there is no question of pleasure!

Respect your hunger, make up with food, feel full, and cope with emotions without eating - these are the four spokes of our imaginary wheel. Another spoke includes the rejection of a dietary way of thinking. If the dietary way of thinking is still with you, then during eating, you either do not choose the food that promises the greatest satisfaction, or you choose it but condemn yourself for eating it.

Chapter 10: Relaxation Techniques

Since we have seen that emotions are the first obstacle to a healthy and correct relationship with food, we are going to look specifically at the most suitable techniques to appease them. Not only is that, these techniques very important to make hypnosis deeply effective in order to achieve the desired goals.

In fact, autogenic training is one of the techniques of self-hypnosis. What does self-hypnosis mean? As the word suggests, it is a form of self-induced hypnosis. Beyond the various techniques available, all have the objective of concentrating a single thought object. To say it seems easy, but it is incredible how, in reality, our mind is constantly distracted and even overlaps distant thoughts between them. This leads to emotional tension with repercussions on everyday life.

Other self-hypnosis techniques that we will not deal with in-depth include Benson's and Erickson's.

Benson's is inspired by oriental transcendental meditation. It is based on the constant repetition of a concept in order to favor a great concentration. Specifically, he recommends repeating the word that evokes the concept several times. It is the easiest and fastest technique ever. It really takes 10-15 minutes a day. Just because it's so simple doesn't mean it's not effective. And you will also need to familiarize yourself with it. Especially for those who are beginners with self-hypnosis. In fact, this could be the first technique to try right away to approach this type of practice.

You sit with your eyes closed in a quiet room and focus on breathing and relax the muscles. Therefore continually think about the object of meditation. If your thought turns away, bring it back to the object. To be sure to practice this self-hypnosis at least 10 minutes, just set a timer.

Erickson's is apparently more complex. The first step involves creating a new self-image that you would like to achieve. So we start from something we don't like about ourselves and mentally create the positive image that we would like to create.

In our specific case, we could start from the idea of us being overweight and transform that idea into an image of us in perfect shape, satisfied with ourselves in front of the mirror.

Then we focus on three objects around the subject, then three noises and finally three sensations. It takes little time to concentrate on these things. Gradually decrease this number. Therefore 2 objects, 2 noises, and 2 sensations. Better if the objects are small and bright and unusual sensations, which are hardly paid attention. For example, the feeling of the shirt that we wear in contact with our skin. You get to one, and then you leave your mind wandering. We take the negative image we have and calmly transform it mentally into the positive one. At the end of this practice, you will feel great energy and motivation.

Autogenic Training

Autogenic training is a highly effective self-induced relaxation technique without external help. It is called "training" because it includes a series of exercises that allow the gradual and passive acquisition of changes in muscle tone, vascular function, cardiac and pulmonary activity, neuro-vegetative balance and state of consciousness. But don't be frightened by this word. His exercises do not require a particular theoretical preparation nor a radical modification of one's habits. Practicing this activity allows you to live a profound and repeatable experience at all times.

Autogenic means "self-generating," unlike hypnosis and self-hypnosis, which are actively induced by an operator or the person himself.

In essence, the goal is to achieve inner harmony so that we can best face the difficulties of everyday life. It is a complementary tool to hypnosis. The two activities are intertwined. Practicing both of them allows a better overall experience. In fact, hypnosis helps well to act directly on the subconscious. But in order for hypnosis to be effective, it is necessary to have already prepared an inner calm such that there is no resistance to the instructions given by the hypnotherapist. The origins of autogenic training are rooted in the activity of hypnosis. In the latter, there is an exclusive relationship between hypnotist and hypnotized. Those who are hypnotized must, therefore, be in a state of maximum receptivity in order to be able to reach a state of constructive passivity in order to create the ideal relationship with the hypnotist.

Those who approach autogenic training and have already undergone hypnosis sessions can deduce the main training guidelines from the principles of hypnosis. The difference is that you become your own hypnotist. You must, therefore, assume an attitude of receptive availability towards you. Such activity also allows a higher spiritual introspection, feeling masters of one's emotional state.

This undoubtedly brings countless advantages in everyday life.

So I usually suggest everyone try a hypnosis session and then do a few days of autogenic training before they start using hypnosis again on a daily basis. It's the easiest way to approach the relaxation techniques on your own and start to become familiar with the psycho-physical sensations given by these practices. Mine is a spontaneous suggestion. If you have tried meditation and relaxation techniques in the past you can also go directly into guided hypnosis. In any case, autogenic training can be useful regardless of the level of familiarity with these practices. It is clear that if you have little time in your days, it makes no sense to put so much meat on the fire. Let's remember that they are still relaxation techniques. If we see them too much as "training," we could associate obligations and bad emotions that go against the principle of maximum relaxation. So I'm not saying do autogenic training and hypnosis every day, 10 push-ups, crunches, and maybe yoga, and then you will be relaxed and at peace with your body. This approach is not good. It is about finding your balance and harmony in a practice that has to be pleasant and deliberate.

Basic Autogenic Training Exercises

The basic exercises of the A.T. are classically divided into 6 exercises of which 2 fundamental and 4 complementary. Before the 6 exercises you practice an induction to calm and relaxation, while at the end a recovery and then awakening.

These exercises are considered as consecutive phases to be carried out in each session. It is not mandatory to carry out all the steps together. Especially initially each exercise will have to be understood individually. But if you intend to stop, for example, in the fourth exercise, and not do all of them, you will necessarily have to do the other 3 exercises in the same session first. The duration of the session remains unchanged, however, because when you add exercises, you will make each phase last less.

First exercise - "The heaviness." It s a very useful exercise to overcome psychophysical problems related to muscular tensions that derive from emotional tensions.

Second exercise - "The heat." It serves to relieve circulatory problems, in all cases where there is a problem of reduced blood flow to the extremities.

Third exercise - "The heart." It is a highly suggestive exercise that allows you to regain contact with that part of the body that we traditionally deal with emotions.

Fourth exercise - "The breath." It produces a better oxygenation of the blood and organs.

Fifth exercise - The solar plexus. It helps a lot of those who suffer from digestive problems.

Sixth exercise - The Fresh Forehead. Produces a brain constriction vessel that can be very useful to reduce headaches, especially if linked to physical or mental overload.

Recommended positions.

The following positions are suitable for both autogenic training and hypnosis and relaxation techniques in general. I suggest initially to use the lying down position and to use it later in hypnosis for virtual gastric bandaging in order to simulate the position on the surgical couch.

Lie Down.

This position, at least at the beginning, is the most used for its comfort. You lie on your back (face up) and your legs slightly apart with your toes out. The arms are slightly detached from the torso and are slightly bent. The fingers are detached from each other and slightly arched.

On the Armchair

You sit with a chair attached to the wall. Your back is firmly against the backrest, and your head rests against the wall. You can place a cushion between your head and the wall.

Alternatively, you can use a high chair to rest your head-on. Legs should be flexed at 90 degrees with the feet firmly resting on them. The tips of the feet should be placed on the outside. The arms should be resting on the supports (where present) or on the thighs.

If there are supports, the hands should be left dangling.

If they are not present, the hands are resting on the legs, and the fingers are separate.

Position of the coachman

This position allows you to be seated but without particular basic support. It can be practiced wherever you have something to sit on (a chair, a stone, a stool...).

You sit, for example, on the chair very far forward without leaning forward with your back.

Your feet must be firmly on the ground, with the tips pointing outwards. Your back should bend forward by resting your forearms on your thighs and letting your hands dangle between your legs so that they do not touch each other. Pivot your neck forward as much as possible, and relax your shoulders and jaw.

Other suggestions

To achieve the best results, the environment must be quiet, the phone and any form of technological distraction must be disconnected beforehand. In the room, there must be a very soft light with a constant temperature that allows neither hot nor cold. The environmental conditions, in fact, influence our mood, and the acquisition of a correct position guarantees an objective relaxation of all the muscles.

It is advisable not to wear clothes that tighten or bother you during the exercises: for this purpose also remove the watch and glasses and loosen the belt.

It goes without saying that constancy is very important for achieving a psychic balance. It only takes 10 minutes a day, but a real reluctance is to be taken into consideration. Before doing this practice, you really need to give yourself some time. It must be deliberate practice. This is one of the reasons why it is not advisable to practice it in small time gaps between commitments, but rather in dedicated time slots.

Also, it is advisable not to practice the exercises immediately after lunch to avoid sleep. At the end of each workout, perform awakening exercises except for the evening just before going to sleep.

At first, checking the relaxation of the various parts of the body will require some reflection. But over time and practice, everything will become more instinctive. Do not expect great results in the first days of practice. Do not abandon the practice immediately because like anything else you cannot expect to know how to do it immediately.

One last tip is to not be too picky when it comes to checking the position to take. In fact, the indications provided are broad; it is not necessary to interpret them rigidly. It must be as natural as possible, so look for what makes you feel better.

YOUNAN CAMPBELL

Chapter 11: Meditation for a Mindfulness Diet

One of the best ways to transition into a diet that's centered around weight loss is to do so using mindful eating. All too often, we eat well beyond what is needed, and this may lead to unwanted weight gain down the line.

Mindful eating is important because it will help you appreciate food more. Rather than eating large portions just to feel full, you will work on savoring every bite.

This will be helpful for those people who want to fast but need to do something to increase their willpower when they are elongating the periods in between their mealtimes. It will also be very helpful for individuals who struggle with binge eating.

Portion control alone can be enough for some people to see the physical results of their weight-loss plan. Do your best to incorporate mindful eating practices in your daily life so that you can control how much you are eating.

This meditation is going to be specific for eating an apple. You can practice mindful eating without meditation by sharing meals with others or sitting alone with nothing but a nice view out the window. This meditation will still guide you so that you understand the kinds of thoughts that will be helpful while staying mindful during your meals.

Mindful Eating Meditation

You are now sitting down, completely relaxed. Find a comfortable spot where you can keep your feet on the ground and put as little strain throughout your body as possible. You are focused on breathing in as deeply as you can.

Close your eyes as we take you through this meditation. If you want to actually eat an apple as we go through this, that is great. Alternatively, it can simply be an exercise that you can use to envision yourself eating an apple.

Let's start with a breathing exercise. Take your hand and make a fist. Point out your thumb and your pink. Now, place your right pinky on your left nostril. Breathe in through your right nostril.

Now, take your thumb and place it on your right nostril. Release your pink and breathe out through your nostrils. This is a great breathing exercise that will help to keep you focused.

While you continue to do this, breathe in for one, two, three, four, and five. Breathe out for six, seven, eight, nine, and 10. Breathe in for one, two, three, four, and five. Breathe out for six, seven, eight, nine, and 10.

You can place your hand back down but ensure that you are keeping up with this breathing pattern to regulate the air inside your body. It will allow you to remain focused and centered now.

Close your eyes and let yourself to become more relaxed. Breathe in, and then out.

In front of you, there is an apple and a glass of water. The apple has been perfectly sliced already because you want to be able to eat the fruit with ease. You do not need to cut it every time, but it is nice to change up the form and texture of the apple before eating it.

Breathe in for one, two, three, four, and five. Breathe out for six, seven, eight, nine, and 10.

Now, you reach for the water and take a sip. You do not chug the water as it makes it hard for your body to process the liquid easily. You are sipping the water, taking in everything about it. You are made up of water, so you need to constantly replenish yourself with nature's nectar.

You are still focused on breathing and becoming more relaxed. Then, you reach for a slice of apple and slowly place it in your mouth. You let it sit there for a moment, and then you take a bite.

It crunches between your teeth, the texture satisfying your craving. It is amazing that this apple came from nature. It always surprises you how delicious and sweet something that comes straight from the earth can be.

You chew the apple slowly, breaking it down as much as you can. You know how important it is for your food to be broken down as much as possible so that you can digest it. This will help your body absorb as many vitamins and minerals as possible.

This bit is making you feel healthy. Each time you take another bite, it fills you more and more with the good things that your body needs. Each time you take a bite, you are making a decision in favor of your health. Each time you swallow a piece of the apple, you are becoming more centered on feeling and looking even better.

You are taking a break from eating now. You do not need to eat this apple fast. You know that it is more important to take your time.

Look down at the apple now. It has an attractive skin on the outside. You wouldn't think by looking at it about what this sweet fruit might look like inside. Its skin was built to protect it. Its skin keeps everything good inside.

The inside is white, fresh, and very juicy. Think of all this apple could have been used for. Sauce, juice, and pie. There are so many options when it comes to what this apple may have become. Instead, it is going directly into your body. It is going to provide you with the delicious fruit that can give you nourishment.

You reach for your glass of water and take a long drink. It is still okay to take big drinks. However, you are focused now on going back to small sips. You take a drink and allow the water to move through your mouth. You use this water not just to fill your body but to clean it. Water washes over you, and you can use it in your mouth to wash things out as well.

You swallow your water and feel it as it begins to travel through your body. You place the water down now and reach for another apple slice.

You take a bite, feeling the apple crunch between your teeth once again. You feel this apple slice travel from your mouth throughout the rest of your body. Your body is going to work to break down every part of the apple and use it for nourishment. Your body knows how to take the good things that you are feeding it and use that for something good. Your body is smart. Your body is strong. Your body understands what needs to be done to become as healthy as possible.

You are eating until you are full. You do not need to eat any more than what is necessary to keep your body healthy. You are only eating things that are good for it.

You continue to drink water. You feel how it awakens you. You are like a plant that starts to sag once you don't have enough water. You are energized, hydrated, and filled with everything needed to live a happy and healthy life.

You are still focused on your breathing. We will now end the meditation, and you can move onto either finishing the apple or doing something relaxing.

You are centered on your health. You are keeping track of your breathing. You feel the air come into your body. You also feel it as it leaves. When we reach zero, you will be out of the meditation.

Twenty, 19, 18, 17, 16, 15, 14, 13, 12, 11, 10, nine, eight, seven, six, five, four, three, two, one.

Chapter 12: Hypnosis portion control session

Is portion control difficult to maintain?

Yes, if you're not mindful about what you put in your mouth. If you've ever heard about the saying, "Too much of anything is not good for you," you should know by now that it's the truth, right?

After you've eaten something small or a large meal, you should ask yourself, "How did that meal make me feel? Does my body appreciate it, and will it benefit me in any possible way other than ensuring I'm full?"

Buffet meals at restaurants have become a popular occurrence. Just why do people feel the need to eat as much as they do?

Most therapists would emphasize the fact that their clients and people, in general, have underlying issues that result in bad habits, like overeating, to either forget or overcome emotional baggage, feelings, and unresolved issues.

It doesn't matter what your reasons may be, overeating is not considered healthy, and apart from causing your body to gain weight, it can affect your body negatively. It can also contribute to health issues, which can be recognized with symptoms, such as indigestion, feeling uncomfortably full regularly, water retention, and higher than average visceral fat in the abdominal region.

Needless to say, habits are in control of our lives, and we are more prone to overeating than we'd like to admit. The U.S. is the perfect example of a country that has created a culture around normalizing portions that are far too large for a person to consume. However, it is the norm and has contributed to over half of the country's residents suffering from either obesity or being overweight.

What people need to understand is that obesity isn't considered a body type. It is considered a severe health problem that can cause countless other health issues. These health issues include heart disease, stroke, diabetes, high blood pressure, cancer, gallbladder disease, gallstones, gout, osteoarthritis, and breathing difficulties, including sleep apnea and asthma.

The reason why portion control is considered difficult is that we eat for all the wrong reasons.

Society is prone to gravitate toward foods that have an unbalanced level of sugar, sodium, unhealthy fats, and caloric content. These foods are also branded more appealing and are promoted wherever we feast our eyes accordingly. People are also used to overeating and have come to adopt it as a bad habit they can't seem to get rid of. Often people also convince themselves that they either can't waste food or feel forced to finish whatever they have on their plate. Other than that, overeating has become perceived as normal. Given that people are more bored, depressed, or emotionally disrupted than ever before, including lazy, eating whatever they can find or opting for the bad option always seem like the best option.

Portion control plays a very important role in our well-being, as it can differentiate us from being healthy or unhealthy. It affects our bodies contributing to how much we weigh and makes us hold on to excess weight. If you're following some type of 'healthy' diet and a reasonable workout routine, always go back and check whether you're eating either enough or too much and if you are being mindful of your eating habits.

Controlling your portions doesn't only account for a slimmer body, but it also gives you more energy and boosts your metabolism. The more food you feed your body, the harder it must work to digest it, which is also why you may feel sluggish and lazy after overeating. Increased food consumption takes a lot more energy and may cause your metabolism to slow down as a means of defending itself against harm.

Hypnosis helps you to rediscover balance concerning you is eating habits, allowing you to become in tune with and focused on your goals. In this way, you will also regain your self-worth, which may have become lost, along with your self-confidence and growth. You can attain all this and more by committing to hypnosis.

Taking it one step further to hypnosis is also thought to be much more effective for weight loss and any type of mind-body commitment, as it has been proven to have a success rate of up to 93% compared to other types of therapy.

That statistic alone should make anyone want to give hypnosis integrated with food control a try.

Although many diet and workout routines are being sold online, some of which are even made available for free, the right approach for losing weight starts with your mind. Hypnosis offers a means of sustainable weight loss that provides us with access to our unconscious mind, eliminates any barriers, and replaces it with thoughts that prove to be more helpful than any type of information. Hypnosis also allows us to dig deep into our minds, almost like we're exploring the files on our computers, and get rid of any negative associations we may have with developing new habits.

Hypnosis for portion control session

In this hypnosis for portion control session, we will be focused on six factors to integrate into your daily life, which will help you make better decisions regarding food choices, as well as the quantity of food you consume. While the goal of this hypnosis session isn't specifically focused on losing weight, but rather in eating less, learning how to control your portions will speed up your metabolism and overall help you experience a better quality of life.

During this session, the six factors we will be focused on include:

1. Focus on eating smart - You will learn how to incorporate a different style of eating that is focused on decreasing your appetite and speeding up your metabolism. This initiative is focused on you eating six small meals per day, which includes a balance of carbohydrates, protein, and vegetables. In this session, you will be focused on creating what you regard as being the perfect day in your mind, in which you imagine yourself eating smaller portions at meals.

2. Focus on shrinking your stomach - Integrating deep breathing into your hypnosis for portion control session, you will be focused on imagining having a small stomach. When you breathe in, you will imagine yourself as having a smaller, flatter stomach. Given that you prefer this image

over your current look, you will be able to trick your brain into thinking that you prefer this version of yourself.

3. Focus on eating slowly - Control your cravings, including sugar and fast-food cravings, as well as eating too much at one sitting. This can be done by imagining a timeline in which you finish your snack or meal. You shouldn't be rushing eating. By focusing on eating slowly, will be able to minimize your cravings.

4. Focus on drinking water - Serving as one of the most helpful tools to reduce cravings and overeating, drinking water to fill up your stomach will play a significant role in helping you overcome portion control. Since drinking water will also help you get rid of ailments, such as stress, fatigue, inflammation, digestive issues, and depression, it will serve you far better than just eating yourself fully.

5. Focus on greens and vegetables - When you're consuming too much food, the chances are that you are eating the wrong types of food. No one wants to eat a big serving of vegetables. That is why filling your plate with 50% of vegetables, and leafy greens is a really good idea to help you imagine that you are still eating enough food visually. You can eat a salad the size of a regular plate for lunch, but you can't eat a plate of fries the size of a dinner plate for lunch. Plus, once you incorporate healthy eating into your daily routine, you won't want to eat as much food because you will learn the value thereof.

6. Focus on the feeling of hunger - During your hypnosis session for portion control, you must acknowledge hunger. If you're not hungry, then you shouldn't be eating, and if you feel like you shouldn't be hungry because you ate a little while ago, drink a glass of water before turning to

food. When you are hungry, however, focus on what your body needs and not what is either convenient or tastes better than a healthier option. Finding foods that are healthy to integrate into your daily diet is also very helpful and important. It could make the difference between whether or not you stick to a healthy eating plan.

The best approach to lose weight and maintain your ideal weight requires you to adjust your lifestyle.

The process is not a quick fix, and different approaches are vital in making it successful. Above all, psychological aspects are crucial in achieving positive results of the hypnotic gastric band. Equally, working out the powerful affirmations and visualization for weight loss is vital. By incorporating hypnosis, meditation, and relaxation you are sure to succeed. With the hypnotic gastric band, you should be aware of what, how, and when you eat.

In intuitive eating, you build trust in your body to remain aware of what, how much, and when you eat. I know it sounds simple but it is worth noting that diet-crazy culture has a significant influence on your beliefs about food.

Therefore, you should ignore meal plans and weight loss prescriptions and become the expert of your own body. It is common to find dieters making short term success in weight loss but failing to maintain their ideal weight. As a result, they feel guilty and discouraged from the approach.

 Intuitive eating fills this gap as it drifts you away from diet culture rules and helps you remove judgment from eating. It guides you to control yourself and be in charge of your eating. Notably, intuitive eating has no rules and the following principles should guide you to weight loss success and crave less food effortlessly.

Avoid diet mentality: Diets are deceiving in promising fast and permanent weight loss. You are likely to blame yourself when they fail. Avoid external control and believe that your own sense of hunger is the only inner control.

Recognize hunger: Hunger is your body's communication that you need to nourish it. Keeping the body fed is key to enhance your relationship with food. Eat only to satisfy your hunger and make it happen as soon as you feel hungry.

Be at peace with your food: Allow yourself to set no conditions to any band. By eating any food, the body takes time to learn that certain foods are no longer restricted. Consecutively, the food stops controlling you.

Challenge the restrictions: Avoid playing by the rules of what you should or should not eat. It means you do not praise yourself after maintaining your calorie limit or feel guilty after eating a muffin. Food is your friend and not your enemy and is key to saturation and energy.

Acknowledge your fullness: If you can tell when you are hungry, you also can tell when you are comfortably full. Your satiety should not be controlled by the amount of food left on the plate but by your internal cues.

Discover the satisfaction in food: In your endeavor to lose weight, you may overlook the satisfaction and pleasure found in eating. There is powerful content and satisfaction in eating what we want in a conducive and inviting environment. The experience makes you realize that you need less food to decide you have had enough.

Do not eat for comfort: Avoid emotional eating to relieve your woes, for it will not make the problem go away. Eating for comfort should not be a mental anesthetic for it can lead to serious health problems. Focusing on other hobbies, taking a walk, or meditating are some of the alternatives to encourage yourself and raise your spirits.

Honor your health: Intuitive eating does not mean that you throw nutrition out the window. By healing and enhancing your relationship with food you are in a better position to incorporate nutrition into your eating choices. Most importantly, when adding the nutrition piece, you should stick it in the respectful self-care rather than diet mentality.

You were born an intuitive eater so you should get back there through internal cues. You should focus on attitudes, changing beliefs, behaviors, and repairing your relationship with food.

Practical guide to hypnosis for weight loss: Hypnosis works by allowing you to change your unconscious thoughts and processes to achieve a specific goal. If you want to lose weight through hypnosis you should influence various beliefs in your subconscious mind about your weight.

These beliefs will help you overcome the perceived impossibilities in losing weight and difficulty in deciding what, how, and when to eat.

Your mind becomes suggestible when in a trance state, enabling you to access and influence your powerful subconscious assumptions. By following this guide, you will find that you have taken some new and positive actions towards the new changes in your own life that you have successfully set for yourself.

Hypnosis Session for Intuitive Eating and Weight Loss

Allowing yourself to relax when thoughts enter your mind you simply choose to acknowledge them then return your attention to the sound of my voice and the sound of my voice goes with you and remains the most important sound you hear.

You feel very proud of yourself you reflect on all the positive things in your life and you know that you will create the most healthy and positive life for yourself and now see yourself clearer on the screen, stomach flat, hips and thighs slim and trim, legs slim and trim, you look great and feel so good you are relaxed and happy, comfortable in your skin and your subconscious mind knows of a time when you only ate to satisfy hunger and you returned now from this moment on to only eat when you are truly hungry.

True hunger and is easily satisfied with small portions of food and embrace change and growth and maintain awareness of the present moment through emotions and feelings in a deep sense of calmness and peace that enables you to eat slowly while aware of the amount you are eating and chewing and feel satisfied from one meal to the other losing weight steadily safely and naturally when you remain aware of what when and how you eat you are confident in the choices you make about how you look so see yourself now walking outside on a bright fresh day perhaps feeling pride and full of energy for the choices you made to eat healthily you radiate vitality and feel fit and slimmer.

You experience your own feeling in a calm and confident state for your health choices and increase your feeling of health and energy and now it is the moment to end this state in a moment I will count back from one to five and you will come up and out of hypnosis bringing all the benefits feeling yourself coming out slowly now one, one, two, three, four, beginning to move and stretch, and five, eyes open wide away feeling good and anchored in each of folding moment of the present.

With the help of powerful affirmations and visualization, you can achieve your ideal weight in the most natural way.

Avoid concerning yourself with what you eat or not but with how you wish to look.

Do not visualize about disgusting eating or loathing some kind of food.

By staying strong and positive affirmation, you make the subconscious mind direct you to eat the right quantities of food with moderation.

Note that nothing happens overnight and you need perseverance and regular powerful affirmation and visualization to experience the effectiveness of a hypnotic gastric band.

Chapter 14: Sleep Better

This procedure urges you to relinquish all your undesirable considerations, pictures, pictures, and profound cell recollections identifying with your weight and identifying with nourishment. In mending these pictures, I utilize the representation of light to assist you with making another light body; a body that capacities in flawless agreement, so your digestion and each and every cell inside your body works in immaculate wellbeing. The greater part of your Hypno Slim sessions will incorporate in any event one procedure called Creating Your Light Body, and where applicable, this procedure is additionally rehashed twice for most extreme impact.

The eight Hypnosis chronicles, in addition to intuitive warm-up work outs.

1. Intuitive Warm-up Exercises

These activities are intended to heat up your subliminal personality before you start tuning in to your HypnoSlim session. Your subliminal personality is that ground-breaking some portion of your mind that we will access during your hypnotherapy sessions; this is the piece of your mind that envisions, that fantasies and that enables you to make ground-breaking, constructive and lasting changes to the manner in which you think, feel and act. Changes that will push you to all the more effectively, and that's only the tip of the iceberg easy make your optimal immaculate body.

2. Unadulterated Motivation

The greatest piece of any effective, enduring change is inspiration. At the point when we hear "change," our mind normally opposes – it's a piece of our body science and not something we can without much of a stretch warm up to. That being stated, this hypnotherapy session will revamp your body's intuitive response to change lastly bond all the fundamental strides to make you wake up and state, "this is the day I venture out arriving at my weight reduction objectives!"

3. Passionate Eating

For a considerable lot of us managing weight issues, bogus hunger is a colossal issue. Obviously, it's simple for thin individuals to state "simply don't eat!" yet when your body's getting every one of these signs about how invigorated and fulfilled it will feel subsequent to drinking that sugar-loaded, charged bubbly drink, or by eating that euphorically liberal chocolate bar – it's extremely hard NOT to give feelings a chance to disrupt everything!

This session will focus on wiping out those bogus food cravings and educating your body on the best way to eat the manner in which you were destined to – eating when you're eager and eating for sustenance. All things considered, how much better do you feel when you've completed that chocolate bar or pack of chips? This is the ideal opportunity you will discharge all the old psychological weight that has been making you clutch your abundance weight. Over and over, I have seen incredible and positive changes happen due to this session. I would need to state this is one of the most dominant sessions of the whole program.

4. Gastric Band

This session offers a progressive new thought in the clinical entrancing field. Similarly, as a gastric band medical procedure takes out abundance weight through substantial alteration – gastric band hypnotherapy works at the intuitive level to assist you with thinning down step by step, aside from without the cost, recuperation and symptoms.

Gastric band trance has been demonstrated to create the equivalent and once in a while preferred results over gastric band medical procedure – without the medical procedure. It may appear to be difficult to accept yet this shows exactly how incredible trance can be with regards to changing conduct and shedding pounds. In this kind of mesmerizing, I utilize explicit systems to retrain your cerebrum in manners that leave it persuaded you have experienced genuine medical procedure and that you have a real gastric band set up. The consequence of this hypnotherapy approach mirrors the aftereffect of the medical procedure. You feel full more rapidly, which encourages you abstain from indulging.

5. Altering the Band

Likewise, with its carefully embedded partner, a hypnotherapy-based gastric band additionally should be balanced. Fortunately, it won't require a touch of cutting, testing or join and once more, is altogether done in the brain. I'll tell your psyche precisely the best way to imagine the band altering as your weight keeps on changing and your frame of mind toward nourishment movements to a solid equalization of control and sustenance.

Simply let my words manage your psyche into a profound, loosened up state so all recommendations are met with zero opposition and the gastric band can work freely to assist you with getting more fit easily.

6. Good dieting

Longings are your body's method for attempting to get something it most likely shouldn't have (like refined carbs, salt, synthetic substances, handled nourishment, and so forth). It's so used to getting what it needs, at whatever point it needs that, similar to a grumpy baby, it will attempt to pitch a fit. It does this not by shouting and beating on the floor, however by flooding your brain with pictures, scents, tastes and a persistent want to make you yield.

Be that as it may, with this hypnotherapy session, you'll not exclusively have the option to step your longings into the ground, yet in addition, supplant those yearnings with solid other options. At this moment, you may not feel that grapes could fill in for chips – however, with the privilege of guided words and feelings saturating your psyche, they will.

7. Exercise Motivator

Truly I'm going to state it; the feared 'E' word. A significant piece of any effective get-healthy plan includes venturing up your degree of physical movement.

Let's be honest. At the point when you return home in the wake of a monotonous day of work, cooking a feast, encouraging the family, tidying up and preparing for the following day – the exact opposite thing you need to do is work out.

Be that as it may, with the intensity of hypnotherapy, you can build your craving and assurance to practice every single day. In this session, you will figure out how to appreciate the expanded vitality that originates from each one of those endorphins moving through your body each time you do work out. Envision how invigorating you will feel when you step up every morning with the longing to move your body in some solid manner. When in any event, hearing, thinking, or seeing the word practice propels you to your very center.

8. Reward SESSION Think Yourself Thin

The more you envision yourself as the slim individual you want to be, the more rapidly this will end up being your world. In this free mesmerizing chronicle you will utilize the intensity of your intuitive personality to truly wash away your abundance fat and make your optimal flawless body

9. Reward SESSION Boost Your Metabolism

Your ground-breaking intuitive personality controls all your body's oblivious procedures, for example, managing your pulse and breathing rate. In this free trance recording, you will go into the control room of your brain to enhance your digestion and assume back responsibility for your body.

Here are some genuine/life viable instances of Hypnotherapy as related by some trance inducer for weight control:

Mary came to me since she needed to get more fit, yet in addition, since she was feeling so wild that she wasn't getting a charge out of any piece of her life any longer. She was scrutinizing the legitimacy of her reality - the monotonous routine of getting down to business at an occupation where she wasn't valued, where she endeavored to profit, in an association with her significant other that was great however not extraordinary and had been attempting to shed more than 100 pounds for the majority of her grown-up life, at any rate 30 years. Mary was an ordinary customer in that she had a go at everything all alone to shed pounds that she could think about that appeared to be sensible to her. There is unquestionably no deficiency of weight reduction plans and projects to be on, and she had attempted every one of them.

She realized how to shed pounds. She'd done it a lot of times previously. Be that as it may, she generally recovered it. What's more, she was burnt out on intuition about it to such an extent. She was baffled about attempting to "fathom" this issue and investing such a large amount of her energy committed to this one part of her life that appeared to have been as long as she can remember center. Mary is great at her particular employment, and knows how to issue settle. She's fruitful in basically each and every other part of her life, yet this a certain something, losing the weight, just evaded her. It generally had. Furthermore, she was so baffled and tired of it that she didn't have the foggiest idea whether it was worth in any event, attempting any longer.

Mary's story had likenesses to other customers' accounts, yet in addition contrasts. Every customer has one of a kind difficulties and qualities they carry with them, and to an enormous degree spellbinding works by uncovering what actually needs to occur all together for every person to be effective. In any case, there are numerous parts of how spellbinding functions that are general, in light of the fact that in all actuality trance is only a word we use to depict a characteristic procedure - a way the cerebrum can center and become mindful, that has been around since human presence. So it's not the spellbinding explicitly that is helping - it's what the entrancing can uncover combined with a comprehension of how the mind and body can cooperate to all the more effectively accomplish wanted results. In this part we will take a gander at how our brain can keep us away from getting more fit, and how entrancing can help move the mind away from unfortunate propensities and negative idea designs into increasingly positive ones.

Chapter 15: Affirmations

An affirmation is a positive statement that reminds you of critical thought. In this meditation below, we have listed a number of affirmations. These are written from a first-person perspective. You can either repeat them back after they are declared or let these thoughts flow into your mind as if they were your own.

We don't always realize just how often we repeat negative affirmations to ourselves. Rather than letting your mind continue to be filled with negativity, look for a way to completely turn your outlook around. You'll want to start to notice the negative things that you say to yourself. These might notice these phrases popping up unsolicited throughout the day: "I am not good enough," or "I am not able to complete this task." These affirmations seem so normal to us now, and positive ones might make us feel uncomfortable. Remind yourself that you deserve to be compassionate towards yourself. Always look for ways to include positive thoughts even if it's difficult to find them.

Throughout this meditation, ensure that you are allowing yourself to believe and understand the statements fully. You can pull some of your favorite ones and repeat them every day, or you can write them down and keep notes around your house so that you stay positive. Look for creative ways to include these affirmations in your life, but most importantly, practice the other breathing.

Affirmations for Positivity

I am a strong independent person. I do not need to depend on anyone. I am able to take care of myself. I am worthy of everything that comes my way. I understand how to get the things that I want from life. I am completely aware of the things that I am in control of. I'm not afraid of the things that are outside of my control.

I am a capable human being who can achieve anything I set my mind to. I will not let the fear of failure hold me back. I understand that sometimes, failure is a part of the process. I am aware of how to use my mistakes to improve as an individual. I do not need to depend on anybody else for my own happiness. I do not place blame on other individuals for my own mistakes. I do not blame anyone else for the bad things that have come into my life. I am aware of the way that other people might influence certain things in my life, but I am not going to blame them for these things.

I understand what I have to do to achieve the things that I want. I am a motivated person. I am able to motivate myself to get things done. I do not look for any outside sources of motivation. I have the ability to self-reflect and motivate myself from within. I will always honor myself and do what I can to look out for me.

I will always respect myself and the goals I set so I can achieve the things that I want. I know how to set goals and my mindset to be a happier and healthier person.

I am somebody who is actively committed to living a better and healthier life. I am always going to look for methods to improve my life. I will always seek out the moments that make me happier.

I am dedicated to doing the right thing. I am focused on getting the things that I want from this life because I know what I deserve. I am not afraid of being an individual who is not going to get the things that I want. I know exactly how to get the things that I desire the most. My ideas are clear. I have clear and realistic goals. I also have realistic expectations for the things that I will get from this life.

I do not hurt myself. Once I do not achieve a goal. I do not punish myself just because I don't get something that I wanted. I do not hurt myself because I am not happy with who I am. I only love myself. I love the person that I am. I use constant compassion to build myself up. I'm able to self-reflect in a healthy way.

I am aware of my flaws, but I do not beat myself up over them. I know the things that I need to work on. I understand my weaknesses, but I do not let these define me as somebody weak. I know how to change my life in order to get things that I want. I will not let these weaknesses hold me back.

I am aware of these weaknesses, and I am ever vigilant of working on them. I understand my flaws and recognize that they make me a unique and interesting individual. I have my own thought processes that are very important to the creativity and uniqueness that I exude.

I let go of all my negative feelings, and instead replace them with positive thoughts. I am able to self-reflect on my negative thoughts in a healthy way, and make sure that I turn them around. I know how to seek out the positive and everything that comes my way. I am aware of the way that I can switch a negative perspective and turn it into a positive one. I choose to be positive every day. I understand what a privilege it is to be able to think within the full scope of your mind. I understand there will still be some days where I can't think positively, but I'm going to commit myself to always trying my best.

I let go of the negative thoughts and emotions of the past. I do not keep myself attached to the toxic mentality that has kept me chained back before. I embrace positivity, and I'm not afraid to be a happy person. I recognize that I am allowed to be happy. I am aware that it is okay for me to be positive. Just because other people aren't positive does not mean that I am not allowed to be.

I can be happy. I will be happy. I am happy. I am comfortable with the person that I am. I am happy and grateful for my body. I understand that I could change things if I wanted to, but I am learning to accept me for me. I do not wish to be anybody else. I hope to change things for the better, but I still appreciate my unique characteristics. I admire other people, but I do not emulate them. I am myself. I am an individual. I have my own important character.

 I am aware of all the things that I want to change about myself. I only have realistic expectations and look to change myself for the better. I am grateful for who I am. I am appreciative of the experiences that I have had because they have shaped me into the person I am today. I accept everything that has happened to me, because if not, then that would mean that I might not be the same person. I still have things to work on, but I am appreciative of the character that I have right now.

All the things that I have experienced have created the person that I am. I am thankful for these experiences because I love who I am. I am happy with the person that I have become. I do not want to know what might have happened if anything else had gone a different way. I'm accepting that this is the reality, and I am not going to try to change it anymore.

I am only looking to build a better and brighter future. I am very aware of everything that I need to do in order to get the things that I want. I am powerful, and I am capable. I am able, and I am willing. I am ready, and I am excited. I am not afraid. I am not frightened; I am not going to let anything stop me. I'm always going to look for a way to improve my life. I am a happy person. Everyone around me knows that I am a happy person. My life matters, and it has value.

I have value as an individual; my character has virtue and will share that with others. I am inspiring to myself and to the people that are around me. I am able to accomplish anything that I set my mind to. I permit myself to be positive, and to be happy. I know that being negative is not going to help me. I know that having a negative mindset is only going to hold me back.

I am aware of all the useful things that I do in this world. I am able to contribute to others and to my own life. I use positivity to get me through the most challenging moments in life. I am able to let go of any negative feelings that might come my way. I make the right decisions and use positivity to get me through. I have a high level of virtue.

I focus on healing my inner child, and I make sure that my choices have integrity. I look for ways to work past my negative thoughts. I know how to get to the root of thought. I know that my past experiences have created the person that I am today. I accept the things that have happened to me, but I do not let them define me. I create my own definitions.

I understand that my situation worked out exactly as it needs to be. I understand that even though something might not be good now that there is a plan, and I will be able to see positivity in the end. Even though not everything might happen for a reason, I can still find a reason for everything that has happened.

I use hope and optimism to expect the best. I do not attach my feelings to situations, so I am not disappointed if things don't go the way I planned. I know that I will still be strong enough to push through. I can use positivity to make sure that I make it through any situation that comes my way.

I refuse to give up because I care about myself. I love who I am, and I'm always going to fight for the best.

Chapter 16: Workout

Getting the Most Out of Your Workouts

Just as with healthy eating strategies, there are important things to keep in mind about physical activity that will help support your long-term success. Let's take a look at a few important considerations that will help you get the most out of your workouts:

Rest days: Even though we haven't even started, I'm going to preach the importance of good rest. Don't forget that you are taking part in this journey to improve your health for the long term, not to burn yourself out in 28 days. Although some of you with more experience with exercise may feel confident going above and beyond, my best advice for the majority of those reading is to listen to your body and take days off to minimize the risk of injury and burnout.

Stretching life: Stretching is a great way to prevent injury and keep you pain-free both during workouts and in daily activities. Whether it's a deliberate activity after a workout or through additional means such as yoga, stretching is beneficial in many ways.

Enjoyment: There is no right or wrong style of exercise. You are being provided with a diverse plan that emphasizes a variety of different cardiovascular and resistance training exercises. If there are certain activities within these groups that you don't enjoy, it's okay not to do them. Your ability to stick with regular physical activity in the long term will depend on finding a style of exercise that you enjoy.

Your limits: Physical activity is good for you, and it should be fun, too. It's up to you to keep it that way. While it is important to challenge yourself, don't risk injury by taking things too far too fast.

Your progress: Although this is not an absolute requirement, some of you reading may find joy and fulfillment through tracking your exercise progress and striving toward a longer duration, more repetitions, and so on. If you are the type who enjoys a competitive edge, it may be fun to find a buddy to exercise and progress with.

Warm-ups: Last but certainly not least, your exercise routine will benefit greatly from a proper warm-up routine, which includes starting slowly or doing exercises similar to the ones included in your workout, but at a lower intensity.

Set a Routine

The exercise part of the DASH plan was developed with CDC exercise recommendations in mind in order to support your best health. For some, the 28-day plan may seem like a lot; for others, it may not seem like that much. If we look at any exercise routine from a very general perspective, there are at least three broad categories to be aware of.

Strength training: This involves utilizing your muscles against some form of counterweight, which may be your own body or dumbbells. These types of activities alter your resting metabolic rate by supporting the development of muscle while also strengthening your bones.

Aerobic exercise: Also known as a cardiovascular activity, these are the quintessential exercises such as jogging or running that involve getting your body moving and getting your heart rate up.

Mobility, flexibility, and balance: Stretching after workouts or even devoting your exercise time on one day a week to stretching or yoga is a great way to maintain mobility and prevent injury in the long term.

This routine recommends involving a combination of both cardiovascular and resistance training.

You will be provided with a wide array of options to choose from to accommodate a diverse exercise routine.

My best recommendation is to settle on the types of exercises that offer a balance between enjoyment and challenge. Remember that the benefits of physical activity are to be enjoyed well beyond just your 28-day plan, and the best way to ensure that is the case is selecting movements you truly enjoy. My final recommendation in this regard is to also include some form of stretching, either after your workouts or on a rest day.

Cardio and Body Weight Exercises

In addition to a variety of different cardiovascular exercise options, the strength-training options you will be provided are divided into four distinct categories: core, lower body, upper body, and full body. Per your sample routine, an ideal strength workout will include one exercise from each of these categories:

Cardio

Brisk walking: This is essentially walking at a pace beyond your normal walking rate for a purpose beyond just getting from point A to point B.

Jogging: This is the intermediary stage between brisk walking and running and can be used as an accompaniment to either exercise, depending on your fitness level.

Running: The quintessential and perhaps most well-recognized cardiovascular exercise.

Jumping jacks: Although 30 minutes straight of jumping jacks may be impractical, they are a good complement to the other activities on this list.

Dancing: Those who have a background in dancing may enjoy using it to their advantage, but anyone can put on their favorite songs and dance like there's nobody watching.

Jump rope: Own a jump rope? Why not use it as part of your cardiovascular workout? It is a fun way to get your cardio in.

Other options (equipment permitting): Activities like rowing, swimming and water aerobics, biking, and using elliptical and stair climbing machines can be great ways to exercise.

In order to meet the CDC guidelines, your goal will be to work up to a total of 30 minutes of cardiovascular activity per workout session. You may use a combination of the exercises listed. I suggest that beginners should start with brisk walking or jogging—whatever activity you are most comfortable with.

Core

Plank: The plank is a classic core exercise that focuses on the stability and strength of the muscles in the abdominal and surrounding areas. Engage your buttocks, press your forearms into the ground, and hold for 60 seconds. Beginners may start with a 15- to 30-second hold and work their way up.

Side plank: Another core classic and a plank variation that focuses more on the oblique muscles on either side of your central abdominals. Keep the buttocks tight and prevent your torso from

sagging to get the most out of this exercise.

Wood chopper: A slightly more dynamic movement that works the rotational functionality of your core and mimics chopping a log of wood. You can start with little to no weight until you feel comfortable and progress from there. Start the move with feet shoulder-width apart, back straight, and slightly crouched. If you are using weight, hold it with both hands next to the outside of either thigh, twist to the side, and lift the weight across and upward, keeping your arms straight and turning your torso such that you end up with the weight above your opposite shoulder.

Lower Body

Goblet squat: Start your stance with feet slightly wider than shoulder-width and a dumbbell held tightly with both hands in front of your chest. Sit back into a squat, hinging at both the knee and the hip joint, and lower your legs until they are parallel to the ground. Push up through your heels to the starting position and repeat. Use a chair to squat onto if you don't feel comfortable.

Dumbbell walking lunge: Start upright with a dumbbell in each hand and feet in your usual standing position. Step forward with one leg and sink down until your back knee is just above the ground. Remain upright and ensure the front knee does not bend over the toes. Push through the heel of the front foot and step forward and through with your rear foot. Start with no weights, and add weight as you feel comfortable.

Romanian dead-lift: Unlike the squat and lunge, the Romanian dead-lift puts the primary emphasis on the rear muscles of the legs (hamstrings). Stand in a similar starting position to walking lunges, but this time you will hinge at the hips and push your buttocks and hip backward while naturally lowering the dumbbells in front of you. Squeeze your buttocks on the ascent back to the starting position. You can also do this exercise on one leg to improve balance and increase core activation—however, you may need to use lighter weights.

Upper Body

Push-ups: These are the ultimate body-weight exercise and can be done just about anywhere. You will want to set up with your hands just beyond shoulder width, keeping your body in a straight line and always engaging your core as you ascend and descend, without letting your elbows flare out. Those who struggle to perform push-ups consecutively can start by performing them on their knees or even against a wall if regular push-ups sound like too much.

Dumbbell shoulder press: A great exercise for upper-body and shoulder strength. Bring a pair of dumbbells to ear level, palms forward, and straighten your arms overhead.

Full Body

Mountain climbers: On your hands and feet, keep your body in a straight line, with your abdominal and buttocks muscles engaged, similar to the top position of a push-up. Rapidly alternate pulling your knees into your chest while keeping your core tight. Continue in this left, right, left, right rhythm as if you are replicating a running motion. Always try to keep your spine in a straight line.

Push press: This is essentially a combination move incorporating a partial squat and a dumbbell shoulder press. Using a weight that you are comfortable with, stand feet slightly beyond shoulder width, with light dumbbells held in a pressing position. Descend for a squat to a depth you feel comfortable with, and on the ascent simultaneously push the dumbbells overhead.

Burpee (advanced/optional): This is a classic full-body exercise that is essentially a dynamic combination of a push-up, a squat, and a jump. This particular exercise is very effective but may be challenging for some and should be utilized only by those who feel comfortable. The proper sequencing of the movement involves starting from a standing position before lowering into a squat, placing your hands on the floor, and jumping backward to land on the balls of your feet while keeping your core strong. Jump back to your hands and jump again into the air, reaching your hands upward.

Chapter 17: How to practice everyday

For your quick workout routine, walk up through the stairs at the office. Park your car at the farthest spot and trek all the way distance. Take your dog on a long walk. Participate in every way you can. That is the goal of exercising. If you miss any workout or you couldn't get going one day, don't just hang up on it, just get back on track the next day.

Set a routine for everyday hypnosis meditation and affirmation for weight loss

If you are stuck in the same old aerobics classes, then you could mix things up and try to take a new class at your gym. Some of the hottest gym classes that you could take include indoor cycling, boxing based programs, yoga classes acrobatics, and martial art. This will help you to be able to combat boredom, which is the number one reason why you participate in emotional eating and quit exercising. Try always to drink a lot of water while exercising. Warm-up before exercising. If you haven't warmed up, then you have to get into the habit of warming up before every exercise. Make it a habit to warm up. It isn't necessary to warm up before any strenuous exercise, but by doing so, you'll be able to get your blood flowing, and you be able to prepare yourself for any activity ahead.

Standing Reach Stretch

One of the stretching exercises that you can do is the standing reach stretch. This stretch involves the upper body's movement. So start with your arms, keep your arms straight down, besides your body with your palms facing backward. Use one arm, raise it forward, and raise it up as high as possible. Now tighten your abs and use the opposite arm to touch your shoulders and stretch across your chest slightly. Now hold the stretch for 10 to 30 seconds.

Repeat the same stretch with your arms reaching in the opposite direction. The neck stretches the chest and backstretch. Use your hands to grab the ends of a small towel in both hands. Now bring your arms to the chest level and slightly tuck on the ends of the towel and hold it for about 10 to 30 seconds.

Neck Stretch

 Neck stretch is the upper-body stretch. This stretch is very good for golfers. Grab the end of a small towel with your end and slightly tuck them to the end of the wall.

The chest and Shoulders stretch

Now the next stretch is the chest and shoulder stretch. This stretch is great after swimming. So take your hands behind you, and hold the end of a towel at your hip. Now raise your chest high and raise your arms forward now hold the stretch for about 30 seconds.

Quadriceps Stretch

The next stretch is the quadriceps stretch. This stretch is good for runners, high-cut cyclists, and walkers. Sit behind the chair and hold onto the chair for balance and support. Now take one hand and grab your other ankle. Gently push your foot forward towards your gluts. Do not tuck or lean forward but keep your chest lifted high. Now do this stretch for about 10 to 30 seconds. Now repeat the same thing using the other leg.

Standing outer thigh stretch

Stand behind the chair, and hold onto the back of the chair for balance. Place one of your feet behind the chair and diagonally press your heels to the floor. Hold the stretch for about 30 seconds and put it doing using your other leg.

Tendon Stretch Arms Lenght

The next stretch is the tendon stretch stand. Keep your arm's length behind the chair and hold onto the back of the chair to support and balance yourself. Now keep your feet a few inches apart from your toes why you point your heels to the ground. Slowly push your pelvis while bending your elbows and leaning forward. Support yourself with your hands to the back of the chair. Now do this for about 30 seconds.

Standing thin stretch stand

The next stretch the standing shin stretch. Stand at the back of a chair and hold the back of the chair for support and balance. Bend your nails slightly and raise the toes of your feet off the ground while resting on your heels. Do this stretch for about 30 seconds.

Hip Stretch

The next one is the hip stretch. Stand at the back of a chair for support and balance while bending your nails across and cross one ankle over the opposite leg. Now sit back watch and hold it straight for about 30 seconds. Repeat the stretch, crossing the other ankle over the opposite knee.

Upper back Stretch and shoulder stretch

The next one is upper backstretch and shoulder stretch. This stretch is perfect for activities that require the upper body and bending movements. So, to begin the stretch, stand behind the chair and hold onto the back of the chair for support. Then take one step away from the chair until your arms are fully stretched. Now move and bend forward from your waist and stretch your shoulders forward, then hold onto the knee for about 30 seconds.

Try to stretch as many ways as you can; the more stretches that you do, the more likely, you will be to avoid tight muscles, prevent injuries, and feel better if your muscles are tight, patient with it. It will take some time for your muscles to go back to their normal length. Stretching throughout your life will help to reduce the effect of aging and will help me to lose weight and reduce the wear and tear of your joints and tissue.

Studies have shown that it is possible to maintain your flexibility through a wide-stretching program that you can follow. You should remember that stretching is not a contest, you shouldn't compare yourself with other people because everybody is different. Some days you might be feeling bar where are some days you might feel tighter.

Stay comfortably within your limits and allow the flow of your energy to come through you.

Now let us look talk about some simple exercises that will help you during your hypothesis session.

Abs

The first one is the abs. So grab a bubble chair or a dumbbell and then lay your back on it while pointing your feet straight. Take the weight and extend your arms over it, and then contract your abdominal muscles while lifting the weight up towards the ceiling. Exhale while moving up and inhale while moving downward. Now you should remember not to bounce on the ball. Moves slowly so that your muscles will be tight throughout the entire set also try to bring your weight at an angle and try to push the weight straight all perfectly vertical. Now the equipment that you need for this exercise are dumbbells and exercise balls, whereas the muscles that you are working out are the upper abdominal and the core muscles.

Conclusion

Many use gastric band surgery as a good way to lose weight, and it works to be sure, but did you know it's an expensive strategy that's vulnerable to complications like having a slipped band, acid reflux, constipation, diarrhea, nausea and vomiting, and many more? You have to ask yourself, is the risk really worth it?

What if you found a way to get all the advantages without surgery risk and expense? Believe it or not, hypnosis therapy does this. Gastric band hypnosis is a modern hypnosis technique where you get reminders that you've had the treatment, and surprisingly you'll start behaving and living as if it were real. Hypnotherapy is one of the ways you can lose weight.

As we've shown, this is a drastic measure, but now Gastric Band Hypnosis will achieve the same results without the surgery. Through Gastric Band Hypnotherapy, a hypnotist can trigger a trance and send you advice to make you believe and behave as though you had the operation. Hypnotherapy is a healthy and effective way to lose weight.

Hypnosis is an accepted practice, and it doesn't get the recognition it deserves. Hypnosis dates back decades, and Western society may trace self-hypnosis back to around the mid-1800s.

The use of hypnosis in recovery, pain, obesity, personal and professional issues, sexual disorders, and much more is well recorded, and the results have been nothing less than impressive.

Such strategies of hypnosis help you break the loop, smash bad habits, instantly avoid the mistakes that led you to fatness in the first place, and also give you the will and drive to uplift yourself, change your lot in life, upgrade your self-esteem and more... All weight-gain-related.

What you need to know about weight loss hypnosis methods is that this isn't some mystical all-powerful obesity remedy. Rather, hypnosis stimulates you to help improve your ability to resist the normal temptations that are now your responsibility.

You won't be controlled by hypnosis like a computer until you "come around," you won't get sick from only thinking about pigging out or indulging in the extra ice cream.

Hypnosis offers the extra little drive to fight, hold back, and not succumb to "urge." You'll find the uncontrollable urge now controllable, not so overwhelming and strong. Your impulses will change, and as you achieve further success, you will achieve further confidence and strengthen hypnosis self-suggestion, and so on.

Hypnosis gastric band methods give you the advantage of not strict diets, paired with a deep desire to break the loop and conquer the weight gain-problems. Good luck!

YOUNAN CAMPBELL